W9-ATM-490

THE COMPLETE BOOK OF
BAZAARS

THE COMPLETE BOOK OF
BAZAARS

Dorothea S. Britton

Coward, McCann & Geoghegan, Inc.
New York

Copyright © 1973 by Dorothea S. Britton
All rights reserved. This book, or parts thereof, may not be
reproduced in any form without permission in writing from writer and the
publisher. Published on the same day in Canada by
Longman Canada Limited, Toronto.
SBN: 698-10467-6
Library of Congress Catalog Card Number: 72-76683
PRINTED IN THE UNITED STATES OF AMERICA

ACKNOWLEDGMENTS

The author is indebted to St. Paul's Methodist Church in Hartsdale, New York, and to the Greenville Community Church in Scarsdale, New York, where she learned much of the know-how described in these pages, and to their ministers, who placed their trust in her; to Miss Marion Reitz, who spent a lifetime teaching students to sew and who was flexible, optimistic, and eager to try a new pattern or idea; to Mrs. Louise Baker, an artist par excellence, whose freshness of ideas for posters and illustrations made all the difference; to Marie Steinkamp, whose encouragement never waned; to Bessie Hart, a far-off acquaintance by mail, whose boundless enthusiasm spurred me on; to Hubert Horan, president of the Scarsdale National Bank, who knows how to support a fledgling business with his friendly encouragement; to Beth Pollard of the Association for the Handicapped of Rye, New York, who constantly made me remember to provide ideas for the handicapped; to Tracy and Linda, who showed me what *young* ladies like to do; to my mother and father, who, like most in their category, believed I could do *anything*; and most of all, to Toby, who gave me the time to try.

For the photographs, taken especially for this book, my thanks to Steve Karas of Hartsdale, New York. I also wish gratefully to acknowledge the help of Arthur Foulkes, who executed the patterns and diagrams.

D. B.

CONTENTS

INTRODUCTION

The word "bazaar" has a magical quality because it plays upon our imaginations and brings into focus some of the more basic human instincts: the desire for acquisition, the expectation of "something for nothing," enjoyment through group activity, personal creativity—to say nothing of the satisfactions derived through the support of a good cause and the challenge of meeting the requirements of a specific budget. It is far more encompassing than the overworked but still popular concept of the "boutique." For me, a bazaar always suggests some of the mystery of the Middle Eastern soukh: hidden-away shops with treasures from Damascus, Cairo, Algiers, Baghdad, and places unknown or treasures that originated from no greater distance than a neighbor's attic. More personally, it is a call to arms for my own creativity, and continual wonderment at the ingenuity of human beings in devising products that are intensely appealing to others. And finally, it is the challenge of free enterprise, to see if one can successfully compete for another man's dollar. Women, particularly, feel that it is an enjoyable fund-raising vehicle, and many have written to me to express their satisfaction and sense of fulfillment from working on a successful endeavor. For myself, I love the beginning, the middle, and, in due time, the end of a bazaar, and I manage to keep one going most of the time. Along with making products to sell, dreaming up fund-raising benefits, and trying out ideas, I serve as director of Crafts and Recreation at the Bethel Home and the Nellie J. Crocker Health Center in Ossining, New York, organizations famous for their annual spring and fall bazaars, where I find it a source of constant pleasure to see the results of the creative imaginations of spirited seventy-, eighty-, and even ninety-year-olds.

It is my hope that all my readers will discover some of the same satisfactions I have experienced while putting together a rousing good bazaar. All the products described in this book have been tested recently in the active, sophisticated markets of Westchester County, New York.

THE COMPLETE BOOK OF
BAZAARS

PLATE 1.   Hand-sewn bazaar products, ready for spring.

I

WHY A BAZAAR?

More and more we are discovering that money is tight, sales are sluggish, people are not as generous as they used to be. Contributions are down, and ever more worthwhile appeals are made to our generosity, yet we must, of necessity, be more selective in our giving. At the same time, the needs and requirements for social service and truly good projects are more urgent than ever, and the projected goals seem to grow by leaps and bounds as we face the problem of where we will find the money to achieve our ends.

Repeatedly individual organizations are having to turn to their own resources for fund raising and replenishment of the monies to operate, and we find once again that "God helps those who help themselves." This is the well-founded *raison d'être* behind the usual bazaar.

With imagination and industry I have seen a tiny band of women in a small church in Center, Missouri, raise their sights from a projected $300 to a realized $1,200, and they are now only marking time until they can again make another try; while in Scarsdale, New York, another group of church women thinks nothing of raising $8,000 in a one-day affair. With more hands to help, they can think bigger. But all used the concept of the bazaar.

There are other benefits beyond the monetary. From time to time all organizations seem to bog down in their own tired procedures. Sometimes we all but forget our original purpose: The same people seem to wind up doing the work, nobody has any fresh ideas; membership is on the verge of turning to something new, and loyalties begin to wane. Yet, surprisingly, just as we seem to be wallowing in our own failures while redefining our aims, then is the time to find the looked-for solution, and often that is simply to turn to "something new." I recommend the "something new" even if an organization has to turn its back on a tried-and-true formula that has been unfailing in its success over the years, simply on the theory that *members matter, too*, even though their goals may have been temporarily achieved. If membership is restless, try a new angle, and blaze a new trail!

If your previous successes have been due to one Herculean effort, try a different approach with two smaller projects, preferably extremely varied in nature. For example, if you were famous for your annual Christmas bazaar, switch to a spring strawberry festival, and in the fall, plan a square dance complete with hoedown country food, and sell gingham and calico products.* Or try a gourmet box supper, then a hobby show or craft carnival; another thought might be an apple festival or later on, a fall Amish outing (whose very simplicity might be appealing). Suit the occasion to the lay of the land where you operate. Try a Piney Party if you're in pine-needle country or a Greenwich Village sale for a neighborhood where everyone does his own thing. You might be starting another annual event and receive for your organization a much needed shot in the arm as well.

A small venture with a multiple of possibilities is a strawberry festival. Festivals imply excitement, something doing, somewhere to go. Make sure that yours is all this and more. Arrange with a grower to provide you with quantities of strawberries, but don't let it end there. Sell white summer aprons and shifts adorned with strawberry appliqués (one manufacturer markets luscious ripe embroidered ones†), strawberry-shaped hot pads, summer garden kneeling pads and gloves, strawberry pincushions and Christmas ornaments, cotton print summer clothes with strawberries in the pattern fabric, hats and bibs, and of course, Shortcake with a Flair. Compile a mimeographed recipe folder of successful strawberry recipes to sell with the berries, to spur your customers on.

* See Chapter X under Strawberry; Easter Products to Make.

† See Chapter X, Bazaar Patterns for Duplication.

PLATE 2.   A gay spring strawberry pincushion equally well presented
as a velvet Christmas tree ornament, with hanger.

If you show people what to do with your product, you'll have
no trouble in selling your wares.

Merchandise seashore products from a table decorated with
a large lily pad, and group the animals around it (see Plates
3, 3A, 3B).

Pine-cone products are endless in their possibilities, and many
successful ideas incorporating them at a Piney Party are given in
this book. Sell pine-scented incense at a profit, along with pine-
scented candles, pull toys made from soft pinewood, watercolors
or sketches of piney subjects, and feature 'balsam balm' at your
refreshment stand. This can be beer, coke, soda, or whatever
drink is popular in your part of the country, depending on the

PLATE 3. Instructions for the water lily are shown at right. For directions for duplicating the crab, see Chapter X, Seashore Products.

HOW TO MAKE A WATER LILY

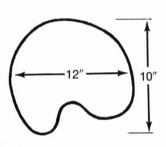

12″

10″

Lily pad—green felt

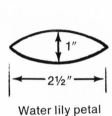

1″

2½″

Water lily petal

Staple petals in center

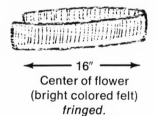

16″

Center of flower
(bright colored felt)
fringed.

Roll up, and staple

PLATE 3A. Salt-water products make handsome profits.

PLATE 3B. Nautical beanbag bazaar ideas (see Chapter X).

weather. Birdhouses and pinewood products are a natural, and signs of products "pining" for a buyer readily come to mind. Seedpod ornaments and decorations could easily be introduced into such a venture. Chemically treated pine cones for color in fireplace flames could be sold in bulk packet (a red burlap bag with a Santa face) at a profit; pine-scented soap is another possibility. An exhibition of interesting pine cones from all over the world could be assembled with the help of the brochure from the Golden Unicorn,* complete to foot-high banyan tree cones from Africa which can be secured from this fascinating supply house. Some sample products in this category are pictured here.

Smaller ventures of this sort do not necessarily demand the expensive decoration and hours of planning required by a large affair. An enterprising outdoor event showing much ingenuity is a handcrafters' tailgate party, held in a large church parking lot. Space for each exhibitor, his station wagon or car, may be allocated by reservation in the parking lot, marked out and identified with simple chalk. Exhibitors may then be arranged in a large circle much as the old pioneers defended their wagons against the Indians, and the burden of sign making and decoration falls on each exhibitor rather than on the committee, a percentage of the receipts going to the sponsors. Such an event is rounded out with a moneymaking refreshment stand, and a corner of the lot should be reserved for rummage and might be called a flea market. This idea has been known to raise as much money as a large indoor affair, one which has been developed for an entire year.

If you reside in Shenandoah Country or in any of the orchard states, where apples, peaches, or cherries make your fame and fortune, put *your* local best foot forward. In seafood country (New Orleans or any coastal areas), offer steaming fish chowders, quantities of oyster crackers, or sand-dollar sandwiches (western omelets served on bread and cooked to order), and eliminate the varied menu required for so many outings. If what you offer is appetizing and good, complicated arrangements only detract from your efforts. A fishpond for children; beanbags shaped like

* See Chapter X, Free Brochures.

PLATE 4.   The Pine Cone Maidens—a table decoration.

PLATE 5.   The shell Angel in Flight ornament.

octopuses or starfish; orange, pink, or red beanbag lobsters or crabs; craft products made from shells; turtles; fish; seals; seahorses; aprons decorated with strings of blue, green, and aqua fish —all make money and carry out your theme.

Tucked away in the Special Projects issue of *Family Circle* magazine in December, 1971 (separate issue from the regular *Family Circle* magazine), was a glorious large stuffed dragon pattern made of calico. If I were working on a seashore products theme, I would make and market him by naming him the Loch Ness Sea Monster (see Plate 3A). The same issue carried lovely patterns for a mermaid and a unicorn. A calico toy boat and Noah's Ark (see Chapter X) would all be useful at a bazaar with a nautical theme.

Many attractive products for bazaar sales are fashioned from shells. A good example of such a product is shown in Plate 5. You will be off and running if you ask your bazaar committee to list all the nautical items you might wish to offer for sale at a profit. Beginning with saltwater taffy, you will be amazed at the ideas which come pouring out—and you'll be on your way.

If none of these themes has yet captured your fancy, here are some suggestions to guide you in developing an idea which will work for your group and for your community. Try to answer the following questions, and a direction will emerge which will lead you into making the right decision for your bazaar.

1. For what local skills, natural sites, or special development is your community notable?

a. arts	f. gardening
b. crafts	g. parks
c. education	h. ecology
d. agriculture	i. historical sites
e. whittling or weaving	j. hospitals

2. What special talents does your group possess?

a. sewing	f. businessmen
b. crafting, sculpturing	g. woodworkers
c. office work	h. knitters and crocheters
d. orchardists	i. general housekeeping
e. skilled workers	

3. What seems to sell well in your community? (What events have usually drawn good crowds?)
   a. fairs
   b. music and concerts
   c. bingo
   d. bazaars
   e. benefits
   f. outdoor events
   g. picnics
   h. church-supported affairs
   i. community-supported programs
   j. political rallies
   k. school-sponsored projects
4. On what holidays do people wish to be entertained?
   a. Christmas (are people *already* too busy?).
   b. Easter (is this a new idea? Consider it).
   c. Labor Day (last gala holiday before winter; back-to-school sales).
   d. Fourth of July (generally good weather; good decorative ideas; patriotism, marches and bands).
   e. Thanksgiving (a horn of plenty in agricultural ideas with which to work; also pre-Christmas sales).
   f. St. Patrick's Day (a natural if your community is Irish).
   g. Memorial Day (summertime ahead with its practical needs. First summer outing. Weather chancy, so plan for indoors).
5. Is your community affluent and especially sophisticated? Or are they middle- or lower-class residents wishing to be amused or entertained?

If they are the former, they will be looking for a novel idea and a sound project to support. They may be away in certain winter months in large enough numbers to influence the success of your event. The same is true of summer months in many communities. By all means, schedule your event when the members of your community are available in greatest numbers.

If you are dealing with predominantly middle- or lower-class people, they may be interested in supporting old loyalties in fixed formats; on certain holidays they will be looking for diversion— and *you* want to be *it*.

With regard to Question 1 (what are your area skills?), if your community has been fervently aroused by the subject of ecology and the preservation of natural resources, a novel bazaar theme might be a beautification bazaar. Tremendous interest can be generated from a group of people who apply their ingenuity toward making "something out of nothing."* This book contains numerous examples of marketable products made from cast-off containers (milkweed pods, pine cones, computer tape rings, cleaning bags, etc.). By using posters, you can inform your public about local ecology with information gained from your local government, and educate as well as decorate.

If your community is one where fishing is a means of livelihood, use that theme as a jumping-off point. Decorate the hall with blown-up snapshots of local fishermen (orderable by mail on submitting a small snapshot to most mail-order catalogues such as Miles Kimball and Helen Gallagher Foster) and generate great local interest by involving your community in its own public relations.

As for Question 2, the direction of your bazaar will be obvious when you consider who your work force will be. It goes without saying that if your group is comprised of workingwomen, your workshops will be conducted in the evening, and you will prepare products to make which can be transported to the home for final completion, in leisure hours, by your membership. This is a *vital* consideration in present-day fund raising.

With reference to Question 3, if life is not worth living for your neighborhood without bingo, by all means incorporate it as a sideline entertainment in conjunction with your bazaar. Push it in your ads, print it on any tickets, call it a Bingo Bazaar if that will help.

As far as holidays are concerned, remember that you want to provide excitement, a place to go, something to do. Decide *when* your community would most like to be entertained. Then *give* it to them!

For final suggestions, don't overlook such obvious old saws as the "You *Can* Go Home Again Bazaar" (nostalgia); "The Cat-Canine Bazaar" (dogs; cats; toys; products; decoration; pet contests; etc.); "The Stars and Stripes Bazaar" (Fourth of July;

* See Ruth Egge, *How to Make Something from Nothing* (New York, Coward-McCann, 1968).

oompah music; bandstand; drum majorette contest; bogus citizen-
ship papers awarded with a kiss at the kissing booth; flags; red,
white, and blue products; etc.); "The Mom and Apple Pie
Bazaar" (*serve* apple pie; *sell* apple pie; all sorts of home-baked
products); use hokey decor and "campy" slogans on your signs,
sell pie plates in the geographical shape of the United States.*
Blush at nothing! Your public will love a real genuine put-on.

Only two absolutes should reign in your imagination as you
plan for your bazaar: Don't forget to *publicize*, and don't forget
to *demonstrate* what to do with your merchandise. To show is to
know—and don't assume a thing. "I thought it was darling, but
I didn't know what to do with it!" is an oft-heard remark at a
poorly run bazaar. Don't allow your group to take your customers
for granted. If you understand this fact of life, you are bound
to succeed.

* See Chapter X, Maid of Scandinavia Catalog.

PLATE 6. A delighted bazaar customer taking a chance on a plush rabbit at an Easter bazaar.

II

SAMPLE OUTLINES FOR SUCCESSFUL VENTURES

1.

A few years ago in a national magazine I stated in an interview that I felt an Easter bazaar made more sense than a Christmas venture for a great many reasons. Among those were some valid ideas which still withstand scrutiny, and I can report that the idea has now really caught on, if the mail I receive is any indication. The most telling argument for a spring bazaar is the availability of manpower for working on the project. For most people, Christmas is a hectic time. Women are pulled in so many directions and their energies are so dissipated for such a variety of reasons that one *more* burden is just too much. This is not likely to be the case in the spring. The doldrum months of January, February, and March are generally dull and uninteresting, so that workshops conducted then offer those who attend something to do, human fellowship, a multitude of bright spring colors to work with—and these are positive factors in any community.

The following are suggestions for a spring bazaar with Easter as the theme, and this fact alone assures you of many ready sales:

Plan A—A Triumphant Easter Bazaar

An Eastertime bazaar will incorporate bright colors and a multitude of handy eye-catching ideas; a sparkling springtime venture.

The bunnies of Hugh Hefner's Playboy Clubs have a universal appeal for the American male; Easter and that magical rabbit

27

PLATE 7. The whole gamut of pastel stuffed animals may be exploited at an Easter bazaar.

have a way of evoking a positive response from the American mother, grandmother, and young child. The whole family will respond to the idea of an Easter bazaar because of the brightness of the delectable pastel colors involved, and when the final event is scheduled, customers will be psychologically ready for a first spring outing, in a buying mood after having been cooped up for the long winter months. You will be proud of your efforts, and the spirit will be catching. These plans were used in a suburban community of 18,000. Work was done by the women of a church congregation of only 100 families, but the word spread about the project, and in the end women of five churches donated their time to workshops. Other communities could expand or eliminate booths and sections according to realistic hopes for achievement.

It is necessary to apportion bazaar divisions into separate units and obtain a chairman responsible for each. Possible divisions, some of which will be discussed later, in greater detail are:

Mushroom Corners (book sale, new and used)
Rabbit Food Bar (restaurant)
Bunny Bake Sale (home-baked goods)
Mr. McGregor's Garden (decorated eggs and Easter egg trees)
Flowers and Fancies (secondhand hats, jewelry)
Tisket-a-Tasket (filled Easter baskets to order; baskets for shut-ins)
Recipe Sales with Russian Pashka Dessert
TV Mix Sale
"I Could Write a Sonnet" Shop (aprons, pot holders, shifts for children)
"In Your Easter Bonnet" Shop (bunnies with hand-knitted sweaters and caps)
Found Under a Toadstool (rummage)
Fishpond, pony rides, games for children
"Purely Visual" (table settings with Easter cards, private collections of eggs, ceramic or candle mushrooms and rabbits on display)

Club members or the church congregation should be asked to contribute, over the weeks, yarn remnants in pastels and other bright colors, braids and trimmings, sequins, beads, used books and hats in good condition, small dixie cups (bathroom size) and coffee tins, rummage, wallpaper scraps, plant cuttings deliverable on bazaar dates, small paper plates, plastic spoons, magic markers, poster board, pipe cleaners, colored felt, black carpet thread, unused Easter baskets, teacups and saucers, and odd egg-cups. Much of this will be donated if signs listing your needs and a carton placed in a convenient collection spot is made available and handy for your supporters.

If possible, find a hardware or paint supplier or hospital food equipment supplier who can furnish white painter's gauze overseas caps in quantity (see Chapter X). With felt-tip pens print date and hours of your bazaar on top or sides of these and give them out to children at local meetings and playgrounds. Children will advertise your function to *other* children faster than any other known medium, for they get around and pass the word with amazing speed. Using posters everywhere, get all the press publicity you can well in advance. A large sign painted on an old sheet strung between two trees and displayed on the premises should go up well in advance of the bazaar. At other scheduled club or church functions publicize your efforts by using one or two of your products on display (after-church coffees, etc.) with appropriate signs: "Our bazaar bunnies wear hand-knit sweaters!"

Decorate the walls and corridors where the bazaar is to be held with Easter themes. Posters describing Easter and its lore and symbols are of interest to spectators: the rabbit, the egg, the lamb, the dogwood tree, the robin, the hot-cross bun, etc. Beautiful decorative pictures can be secured from a single copy of the Easter Ideals Publications (see Chapter X). Two weeks in advance of the bazaar, force forsythia and pussy willow; then hang cardboard Easter eggs (covered with wallpaper or Con-Tact) from the branches, to be used as booth or table decorations. (Scouts or church school classes can contribute these for their part in the bazaar.)

UNITS FOR AN EASTER BAZAAR

Mushroom Corners:

A reading center with chairs provided for small and large readers, selling used books. You might use an outdoor summer umbrella and table to fashion a giant mushroom by wrapping the stem and top of the umbrella in layers of old white sheeting, shaping and pleating the undersides with staples. Large red paper dots glued to the top give a very realistic look to your mushroom. Stuffed animals, bunnies, chicks, ducks, frogs can be sold from this area (see Chapter X). If the booth chairman has the stuffed toys, pot holders, etc. precut and placed in Baggies, women in the congregation will pick them up one Sunday and return them completed on the next.

Rabbit Food Bar:

Brunch, luncheon, and dinner served by men of organization or church. Proximity to kitchen facilities is a *must*; keep the menu limited but good. Example: coffee and doughnuts for brunch for early buyers; hot dogs, sandwiches, coleslaw, coffee for lunch or dinner. Using cardboard and waterproofed paint-

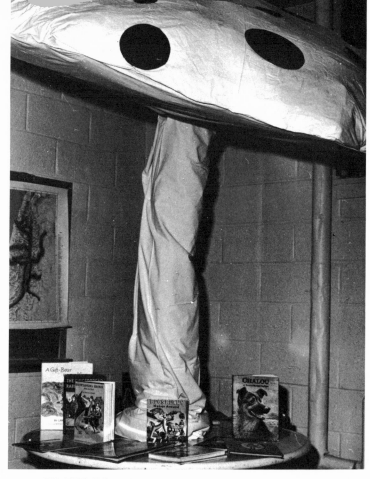

PLATE 7A. A giant mushroom from a garden umbrella.

mixing pails as containers, serve free carrot strips as relishes from the center of each table (covered with flowered Con-Tact these provide color and decoration). Peanut butter and jelly sandwiches can be made well in advance and frozen until the day of the bazaar. When sandwiches are made, decoration can be introduced by using both whole wheat and white bread. With a cookie cutter, cut a rabbit shape out of the center of a whole wheat slice for the top of the sandwich. Save this cutout and interchange with cutouts from white bread top slice. The tops of your sandwiches will then have interest and decoration.

Recipe Sale:
In close proximity to the Rabbit Food Bar feature a dessert sampling booth where recipes are sold. Using bright Easter colors, make a sign advertising a glamorous, traditional Russian Easter dessert and confection—the pashka, sure to provide interest because it's made in a flowerpot (see Chapter IX). Using tiny paper plates and spoons, offer samples, perhaps even a demonstration when new pashka is being served. Displayed on china or glass pedestal epergne, it is a culinary triumph. Mimeographed recipes sell for 25 cents in booklet form.

TV Mix Table:
TV mix is made by a committee in church kitchens prior to the bazaar, packed in Baggies for freshness and sold from accumulated coffee tins which have been decorated with flowered Con-Tact. The recipe can be found on Corn or Rice Chex boxes. This is always well received.

Mr. McGregor's Garden:
The most appealing, eye-catching, and best-selling items which can be offered at an Easter bazaar are small and large hand-decorated Easter egg trees in papier-mâché pots. They will require the largest portion of your supply purchasing funds, but will spread your fame far and wide, for everyone who sees one wants one. Eggs must be jeweled and braided, and hangers attached; papier-mâché pots must be started from scratch to keep costs down. But what a satisfying feeling of accomplishment when you've mastered these beauties! Each small tree requires five to seven pieces of foliage, one tree shape, five decorated eggs, two butterflies, one tiny bird, a small amount of aqua sparkle grass to cover the base of the tree, which has been grounded in plaster of paris. The tree or branch is ordered from the Pink Sleigh catalog. Each branch is 25 cents (see Chapter X). The foliage is sold by the bag and will make many small trees. Each piece of foliage has a loop for easy attachment to the tree. Sparkle grass is also sold by the bag. Pots require commercial papier-mâché mix, small dixie cups (bathroom size), gesso (a paint surfacer painted on

PLATE 8. A small Easter tree in hand-made papier-mâché pot (directions in Chapter IX).

PLATE 9. A large Easter tree fashioned from a plastic tree trunk and five smaller tree branches.

PLATE 10.   Table decorations for an Easter table at a spring bazaar.

to mâché with a paint brush once it has hardened, available at all art stores), and spray paints in bright Easter colors. Attractive pastel braids are wound around the top surface of the pot, and braid seam is covered at the front center with a glued-on butterfly or jewel (see Plate 8). Directions for papier-mâché pots are found in Chapter IX.

Purely Visual:

If space permits, a roomful of Easter ideas for the general interest of the public adds an interesting dimension to an Easter bazaar. A collection of decorated eggs, instruction in egg decoration, perhaps a table for Easter Sunday dinner with co-ordinated fine china and some of your Easter table products make fine conversation pieces. Patterned sheets provide unusual tablecloths for such a table.

Bunny Bake Sale:

Tips on merchandising food are given in Chapter IV. One

34

PLATE 11.   Incorporate all rooms and hallways for space in selling.

PLATE 11A.   Don't let the decorations overshadow the merchandise.

PLATE 12.   Woodland rabbits in a plastic egg for an Easter bazaar.

piece of equipment easily available to your food committee is a slightly squeezed empty frozen orange-juice can which makes a perfect egg-shaped cookie cutter. Plastic strawberry baskets are an effective container for the sale of cookies.

Suggested patterns for an Easter bazaar would include the small knitted Easter Basket, the Festooned Flyswatter, the Butterfly Light-Switch Cover, the Chick-Shaped Felt Pencil Holder, and the Pastel Felt Bunny Purse. See Chapter X, Easter Items to Sell.

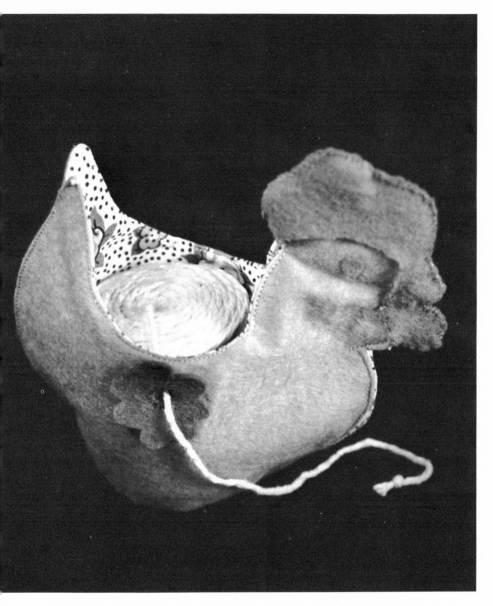

PLATE 13. This kitchen string-holder rooster was developed from the pattern for Floribunda Fowls from *Golden Hands* magazine.

An extremely modern Christmas is not, to my mind, a very good theme for a bazaar. This is not to say that bazaar offerings should not be thoroughly up to date; but nostalgia is one of the strongest features of a fine Christmas bazaar, and a project developed without exploring its nostalgic possibilities ignores an integral part of holiday success. For one thing, people will miss it when they come to see the show; most buyers count on such happenings to evoke the Christmas spirit, and this is precisely what you should aim to accomplish.

Two suggested variations on a popular workable theme are A Country Christmas and Christmas Around the World. The latter theme is extremely ambitious, and the former can be as limited in scope as your resources dictate. Both can be utterly charming in their development and execution as projects.

Plan B—Christmas Around the World
(Reduce or expand to fit the needs of your group:)

WHAT: All's Fair—Around the World (Bazaar)
WHEN: November 18, 1972
WHERE: Northside Methodist Church, Bazaarville, U.S.A.
TIME: 11 A.M. to 8 P.M.
GROUP: Women's Guild of Northside Methodist Church
PURPOSE: Getting to know you, getting to know all about you—our talents, our creativity, our purposefulness in working together in fellowship and harmony for a common goal.

COME STROLL WITH US TO:

A. *Flower Mart Beside the Zuyder Zee* (Green Thumb Booth, featuring fresh plants, garden tools, work gloves, garden baskets, herbs, sachet, etc.).

B. *An Eighteenth-Century Stroll on Duke of Gloucester Street* (antiques exhibited from Bazaarville's finest shops. Consignment of things).

C. *Kris Kringle's Korner Shoppe* (customers greeted by Mr.

and Mrs. Santa who are proudly displaying new toys for the Christmas season).

D. *Brussels Boutique* (creative stitchery at its loveliest).

E. *Chateau de Gateaux* (the house of cakes, pies, and candies).

F. *The Country Store* (strictly Americana, selling jams, jellies, pickles, cheese, handmade items).

G. *The House of London* (decorative items for homes).

H. *Shoemaker and the Elves* (come light the Christmas tree and deck the halls with hand-decorated ornaments. Christmas tree sale).

I. *The Flea Market* (small shops from the streets of Paris).

J. *The Thorn and the Thistle* (MacGregor's Pub—snack shop serving from 11 A.M. to 3 P.M.).

K. *Dinner on the Appian Way* (famous Italian cookery: original recipes, dining with the added pleasure of strolling musicians).

L. *Geisha House* (an elegant boutique for men only. Lovely Oriental women to serve tea and fortune cookies as they assist in the purchase of "that special gift").

M. *The Maharaja's Elephant* (white, of course, and in this shop expect to find just the item awaiting your own creativity to make it a "thing of beauty." Rummage "nearly new").

You will need a chairman for each section of an ambitious bazaar such as this plan suggests. All the units described for this theme, as well as others your group might devise, are possible if your organization has a large membership. The secret of this plan lies in overall organization and the *delegation of responsibility* to individual chairmen. The total effect achieved will then be a potpourri of flavors, truly international, representing the flair and imagination of all the chairmen and individual workers contributing to it. It goes without saying that such a large concept requires a lot of space: a large church or hall, to accommodate all these varied booths and entertainments. The rewards are that you will make a large profit and your customers will have a truly exhilarating and memorable experience.

Church or building corridors are utilized, as well as church schoolrooms, hallways, parking lots, and stage and platform areas. The great American penchant for small boutiques, lofts, and stalls is turned here to your advantage. With this setup the individual chairman can concentrate on making her area an exceptional and unusual thing. Competition enters the picture here, but it can be a healthy expression of free enterprise if everyone gets into the spirit. The enthusiasm and cooperation of the overall chairman can be an infectious and friendship-cementing thing.

Besides the booth chairmen there must be chairmen of art and posters, publicity, banking or finance, storage, and decoration. (The storing of merchandise can be a really extensive undertaking.) Often these categories are best handled by people other than your membership regulars. Their functions are rather specialized, and you can draw your talent from unusual sources. For example, a high school youngster may very well be your most creative and imaginative poster and sign artist. Teen-agers make the best children's entertainment booth supervisors, and they enjoy this activity and can run it well.

Publicity can be effectively handled by a businesswoman who is knowledgeable about press releases; a local newspaperwoman is a natural even though she may not have time to be extremely active in your organization. Above all, she should not be timid; a go-getter is the least you should settle for in this area.

Money and banking are well handled by a man if one can give you the time. It is possible that he may be more knowledgeable about one-day insurance to cover the large sums of money which will be handled in your bazaar area during business hours and for which you should have protection after you have widely advertised that you will be conducting business on that date with the public. Many women are also very informed on such matters. Whomever you designate should be well organized and prepared to have cash on hand for each booth chairman on the day of the bazaar which will be collected at regular intervals as the benefit progresses. He or she will also set policy regarding personal checks, and those wishing to cash them on the day of the bazaar should be referred to the fiscal chairman in order to present proper identification. Therefore, he or she should be seated in a central area where the booth chairman can know he will be available when needed. One or two assistants should be recruited to serve as runners when necessary.

Storage for accumulated merchandise which you have made or acquired may present a problem. A cooperative member whose children are away at college, who is newly widowed, or who for whatever reason has a large house and small demands may wish to contribute by offering that valuable property, space. She may even be willing to pick up and transport, which is no small consideration.

The chairman of decorations may also arrange for a policeman to direct traffic, arrange parking space, consider buildings and grounds, and consider alternatives for inclement weather, as well as decorate the area.

Plan C—Christmas in the Country

A much less demanding but quite charming bazaar can be developed around traditional Christmas symbols; booths representing such concepts as:

A. *An Iowa Christmas* (mufflers, mittens, stocking caps, caps, bird feeders, birdhouses, mailboxes découpaged, donated antiques).

B. *An Early American Christmas* (candles, doll houses, doll clothes, cradles, handmade dolls).

C. *Christmas on the Farm* (cheese balls, ornaments of walnuts, pine cones, sweet-gum balls, taffies, candies [see Chapter X]).

D. *Handmade Christmas* (knitted products and sewing).

E. *The Woman's Holiday* (mincemeat, cookies, dried flowers and herbs, sachets, fruitcake).

F. *The Family* (handmade gifts for Mom, Dad, and Grandma; sale of Christmas trees).

G. *The Wreath* (wreaths of pine cones, lace, cleaning bags, evergreen [see Chapters I and X]).

H. *The Lamb* (stuffed animals, artwork, plaques, nursery equipment, baby clothes, layettes).

I. *The Origin of Christmas* (the manger scene in every medium).

PLATE 14. Some products for a Christmas in the Country bazaar.

J. *Attic Sale* (trash and treasure [donated]. Also articles on consignment).

K. *The Cracker Barrel* (a delicious luncheon of homemade vegetable soup, sandwich, dessert and coffee).

Plan D—The Mini-Bazaar

A very small bazaar may be put together for the purpose of augmenting your treasury and used as a supplementary aspect to a club's regular Christmas programming.

The seating for the program is arranged at the front end of the auditorium or meeting rooms, and then the other half of the premises is given over to a number of tables for a mini-bazaar.

Leaving adequate space between tables, appoint one chairman for each table and allow her carte blanche on its products and decoration. The theme for the entire grouping might be no more elaborate than "The Family at Christmas." One table would feature products for Mom, another for Dad, a third for Grandma, another for little sister and brother, one for the teen-ager, another for pets, and one final table for the family tree. Although extremely simple, this plan is almost infallible because it solves the Christmas shopping problems for your whole membership, as well as enabling them to support their organization.

A mini-bazaar also can utilize the Peace in Our World, United Nations approach suggested by the larger "Around the World" bazaar. There will be people in your membership who will know ethnic customs and skills and will have old-world ties which you should incorporate in this sort of undertaking. Someone of Swedish descent might demonstrate the customs of her heritage, and should be given that table to run. The Chinese or Indian family in your congregation might elect to run their own table, and it will prove intensely interesting to the others.

Some countries and their Christmas customs and the products which could be made for a bazaar table to represent these nationalities are:

> *Belgium*: At Christmas, chimes in the cathedral at Antwerp call the people to worship. There are colorful processions to church, bearing images of the Christ Child.
>
> > *Products to sell*: Lace, wind chimes, bells, Christmas carol booklets, homemade crucifixes, miniature manger scenes (see Plate 15).
>
> *Brazil*: A fiesta atmosphere is apparent here on Christmas Eve, followed by Christmas Eve supper.
>
> > *Products to sell*: Banners and wall decorations (heraldic and Christmas themes and calendars), other religious artifacts.
>
> *Denmark*: One of the prettiest customs of the Danes is their traditional remembrance of the birds and the birds' Christmas dinner.
>
> > *Products to sell*: Bird feeders, birdhouses, bird food and suet, birdcage ornaments (see Plate 28, page 97), *Bird's Christmas Carol* (paperback).

PLATE 15.   A miniature manger scene flanked by two acorn Christmas choirs.

PLATE 16.   Sell a booklet of unusual recipes and show or offer samples to your customers.   The recipe for stained   glass cookies may be found in Chapter IX.

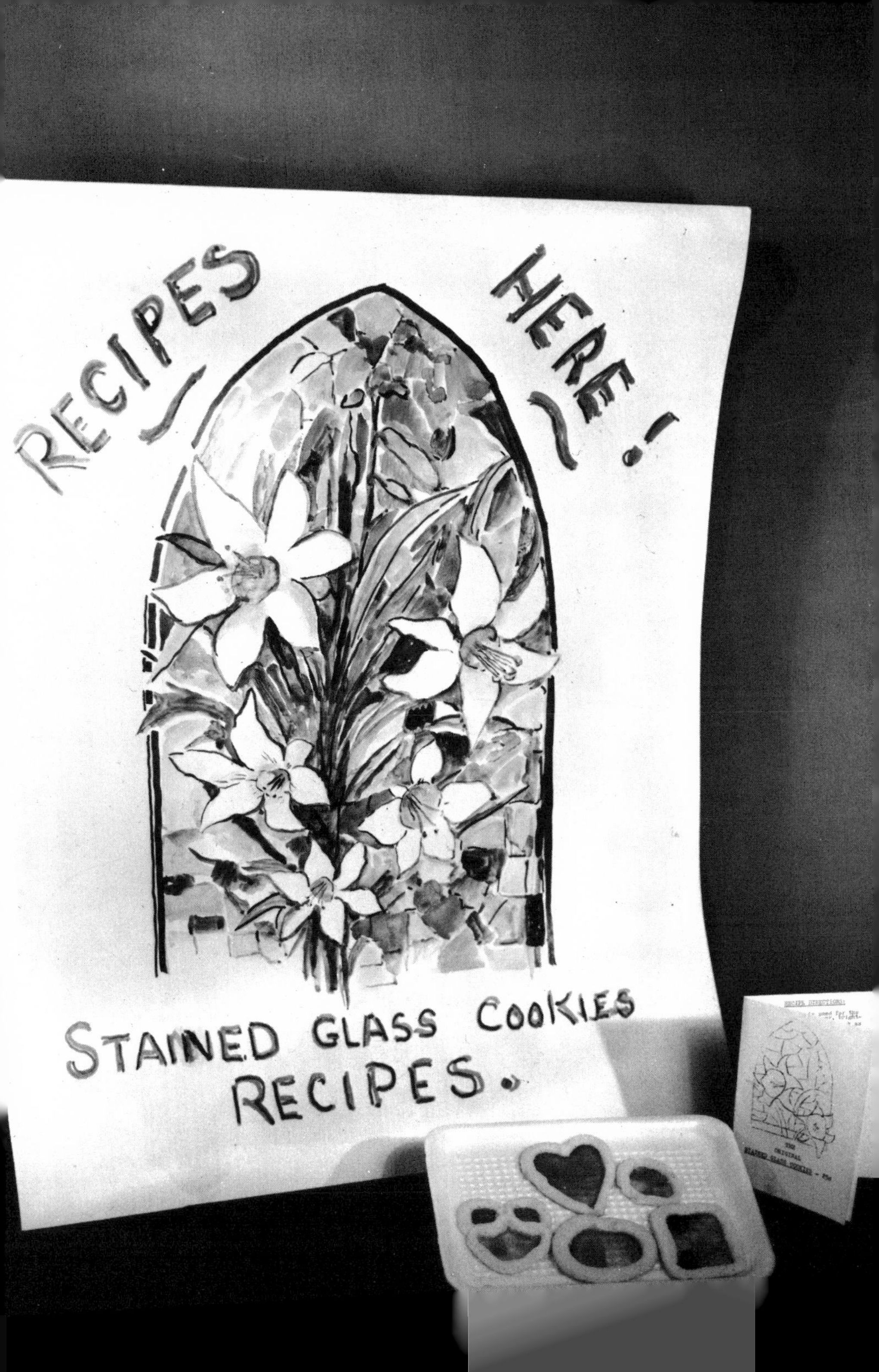
RECIPES HERE!
STAINED GLASS COOKIES
RECIPES.

England: On Christmas Eve the Yule log is brought in to assure good luck for the New Year.

> *Products to sell*: New Year calendars, fireplace matches, hearthside brooms (see Plate 51, page 160), chemically treated logs and flame coloring pellets, plum pudding, *A Christmas Carol* by Dickens.

Finland: On Christmas morning there are church services, tiny candles in the church windows, people arriving in sleighs with tinkling bells.

> *Products to sell*: Star decorations (see Plate 4), stained glass ornaments, cookies, and recipe (see Plate 16), sleighs for table decorations, bells (see Plate 60, page 194).

France: St. Barbara's Day, December 6, heralds the holiday season. Incense is burned; wine and sausages are served.

> *Products to sell*: Incense, wine, sausages, feltwine, bottle jackets, perfume, lingerie, sachets. See Chapter IX.

Germany: Toy giving is an essential part of Christmas in Germany, "O Tannenbaum" is a main source of enchantment: the German Christmas Tree.

> *Products to sell*: Toys of all sorts, tree decorations and supplies, Christmas tree sale (a table might be featured where children would be left to paint and decorate their own wooden ornament with paints set out on table. At a cost to you of approximately 25 cents, charge 75 cents per child, paints and ornaments furnished. See Chapter X, Christmas Products to Make, for supplies).

Greece: Here family reunions and parties highlight the holidays. There is much party merrymaking.

> *Products to sell*: Christmas party decorations, handmade place cards, holiday table centerpieces and decorations (see Plate 4). Festive novelties, candles, etc.

Holland: Christmas means skating on the dikes.

> *Products to sell*: Secondhand skates.

Ireland: Christmas means the time of great hospitality. A cup and saucer are placed on a table in each home for the refreshment of wandering souls from purgatory who are believed to come home for Christmas.

> *Products to sell*: Odd cups with saucer planted with baby tears and plant cuttings, shamrock ornament, kissing booth, polished "blarney stones," Irish lace, etc.

Italy: The *presepio* (manger scene) is found in every Italian home. Shepherds come down from the mountains to salute the Virgin and Child.

Products to sell: The Holy Family statuary, angels (Plate 5), shepherds, lambs, wise men, miniature mangers (Plates 15 and 17), pipes and flutes. Christ Child in the Walnut ornament (see Plate 17).

Mexico: Piñatas are broken in the streets for children's fun.

Products to sell: Piñatas, Eye-of-God ornament, Mexican bags and eyeglass cases, products of straw and tin or silver.

Norway: The preparation of food to be stored for the long winter is celebrated.

Products to sell: This would be a natural for a baked goods table; animal-shaped cookies.

Poland: Puppet shows called *Schopka* depicting the murder of the innocents by Herod are given during the holidays.

Products to sell: Puppets for children, instruction in making puppets, puppets to view. Sale of paperbook *Pinocchio*.

Syria: The Syrian Santa Claus is the camel that brings gifts on New Year's Day. On Christmas Eve a bonfire of vine stems is made in each church area in memory of the Magi who were cold from their journey.

Products to sell: Coins, camels, incense, perfumes.

United States: Candlelight services, Christmas carols, a spirit of fellowship and goodwill, brilliantly lighted and decorated fir trees, excited children.

Products to sell: Poinsettia plants, mistletoe (in Baggies), glistening snow scenes in glass for children, eagle paperweights, Stars and Stripes covers for zip code booklets, stick candy, Americana, popcorn and cranberry chains.

Note that such a mini-bazaar seems to educate your membership and the public, as well as spur sales. More about mini-bazaars in Chapter III.

Note to a Bankrupt Organization

I once was asked to advise a group on community fund raising who confessed to me that their collective bank account was nil. One of their more affluent members offered to foot the bill for

PLATE 17. The walnut half used here as a cradle and at left as a decorative holder for miniature flowers, is a natural container.

the purchase of supplies to run a bazaar. I advised against this, for when they had run a bazaar funded in this way, a disproportionate part of the whole having been contributed by one member, the growth and personal satisfaction aspect of the undertaking would not have been filled for the entire membership.

We solved their problem by holding a sort of organizational garage sale of rummage, contributed by all the members. It was held in a member's garage, and over the door hung a large sign which read:

THE STORE OF THREE WONDERS

1. You wonder if we have it
2. We wonder where it is . . .
3. Everybody wonders how we find it. . . .

Needless to say, they made several hundred dollars toward bazaar supplies and, from that point on, never lacked for club spirit or enthusiasm.

III

ROUNDING UP YOUR TALENT

In every church, club, or organization with female membership, there are some who are adept with a needle, some who have an understanding of crafts, some who can bake or cook and are clever in food preparation, and some who have artistic skills.

Many will disclaim all talent, but after working with numerous local groups at virtually every level, I can report that nothing is so apparent as the tremendously innovative talents of the American housewife. For many, after a lifetime of making do with very little, their industry and imagination are almost beyond belief. Those old saws about the lady of the house running all its machinery with the aid of a hairpin and a well-aimed kick are all based on hard truth! Walk into any good woman's exchange in the United States and see the handmade products devised by some industrious lady who had willing hands and economic or creative motivation. And those who are lacking in imagination are often immensely skillful. Both traits may spring from the most unexpected sources. If you don't believe me, read Mary Gibson's *Family Circle Book of Careers at Home*. There is talent all around you, in every generation. The gal who thought up Mod-Podge in her kitchen to simplify the art of découpage was an Atlanta housewife.

Everyone knows a homemaker with a green thumb. Put her in charge of the Plant Booth. And the lady who makes her own clothes (Sewing); the self-styled interior decorator (Treasure Trove or Articles on Consignment); your neighbor the gourmet (Baked Goods); the gal who reads (secondhand books); the do-it-yourselfer (Crafts); the member who can't get off the phone or the stay-at-home with tiny children (Phone Committee). There's one of each in *every* community. Draw a bead on the gal you want, and tell her why you need her. It's a rare woman who doesn't respond to that approach; I know, because it gets me every time, and it's a common female trait!

In addition, your group will not be normal if it does not also include what I call the difficult people—one or two women who don't seem to get along with anybody. Every group has them. You know what I mean: If *they* like it, you *know* the product won't sell! Put them in charge of pickup and storage, if possible. I do that on the theory that they may tire themselves out and wind up being too weak to cause trouble. It doesn't always work, but it's worth a try!

The Ladies You'll Meet

Any endeavor which benefits the community and relies on volunteered free services and the donation of spare time will always encompass, along with it, a cross section of human nature, its foibles and its strengths. You will deal with women who are overly timid and those who have a downright exaggerated opinion of their skills. Fortunately, there are usually more of the former, and one of the satisfactions you'll have is in observing the pleasure a worker gets as she discovers she's really adept at turning out a finished product. There's a lot of psychology at work in a good production line, and a good chairman learns to praise with genuine enthusiasm, offer a lot of encouraging support, and be philosophical about the shoddy products which inevitably will be slapped together by some less than perfectionists. The only way one can come to terms with these is to keep one's cool and price them in direct proportion to their quality and true worth when selling time comes. Never, *never*, criticize someone's handwork, if it doesn't meet your standards. Time and effort that are donated are precious commodities, and everyone hasn't the same eye for color, line, and perfection. Often I have come close to crying out when supplies carefully purchased were wasted or returned, virtually ruined by an impossible sewing job or a careless pair of scissors. Bite your tongue, and try to remember that the goal you are really after is a united group or congregation, working together, and that the monetary profits you reap are simply icing on the cake. Sometimes a giving, willing heart outstrips the skill of the hands. To hold one's tongue is easier said than done, but if you try it, you'll garner real rewards.

You should be prepared for the various personalities who reside in every community and with whom you will work. For easier recognition, I have divided them into categories or types, and soon enough they will be recognizably familiar:

The "I'm Not Very Creative, So Give Me
Something Simple to Do" Gals, and, Conversely,
the "I'm Just Naturally Creative" Types

The backbone of a bazaar or benefit is the man or woman who says willingly, "Give me something simple to do. I'm not very clever, but I can follow instructions." They really mean this, and sometimes people truly know themselves best. Until you can evaluate them differently, take them at face value. If you are organized, you will have available for them a list of routine procedures which must be followed in the production of your merchandise. Appoint these people to such projects and thank them profusely for contributing to the unglamorous but vitally necessary work.

By contrast, the "naturally creative type," whether or not her self-confidence is justified, usually will be resentful of supervision and suggestion. My advice is to take her at her own evaluation, and bend with her if you can. No one has a corner on ingenuity, and even you may learn a thing or two. I will always remember one enterprising grandmother who beat me at my own game and showed me a few step-saving shortcuts as well. She saved me money, time, and effort. So keep an open mind.

"We've Always Done It This Way"

Tactful Tillie, who insists on telling you how it's always been done in the past and strongly implies it was a whole lot better, is always one of the work force crowd. You may be entirely con-

52

vinced that this is exactly why, in years past, they never did as well as you'd like to do on your current venture. Use your good sense and answer her somewhat like this: "I know they've done some great things in the past, but one of the things I feel we need to try is a new approach. Maybe we'll go back to the old system, but let's give this a try, if only for a change." She'll grumble, but she'll come around.

"My Husband Says"

Listen carefully for those three little words. They can lead to very real support for some of your projects.

One of the most attractive items we ever came up with to sell resulted from some subtle inquiries a wife had made concerning a suggestion by her husband. "You ought to have some of those wooden duck pull toys for little children that I make for our grandchildren," he remarked to his wife. This gave me the lead I needed to approach him to make us a quantity of his specialty, and this he was willing to do. They were a great success and led to some other contributions from men whose women were involved. A handy husband is an asset to be cultivated.

"I Just Know You Could Make Something Out of This" or *Treasures Too Tired to Tackle*

You may be just the housewife who woke up "being chairman" and, after one unsuccessful trip to the local library looking for ideas, were really discouraged. All you found to guide you was a yellow-paged tome, looking like *Popular Mechanics* for 1924 which gaily assumed every household contained a set of fantastic power tools. And this, after everybody just assumed you were something of a genius! Well, the healthiest approach is to allow yourself to be sold on that idea—modestly, of course. You'll find yourself being inventive just to perpetuate the myth. After all, you did go one step further than the rest—you agreed to be the chairman! So trust in someone or something and brazen it out, and some of your lieutenants will make you look good, however undeserved. On every project I've ever attempted someone has piled in and bailed me out once I was over my head. Don't be afraid to admit it if it's happened, and charitable souls will give you credit for having made the effort. Sometimes people don't use their heads very much and bring you scraps to work with that would take divine guidance to turn into something salable. Never, never turn any of this down. Accept it with a smile, always keeping in mind that there is a back door with a trash can at the rear of the workroom. Your donor meant well, and she took the trouble to bring it to you. She'll feel you're "snooty" for sure if you turn her down, and how much wiser to thank her with a smile as you file it all away in the receptacle at the rear of the church, under "Treasures Too Tired to Tackle".

*"You Don't Mind, Do You, If I Buy This
Beforehand?" or
"I Think This Is Overpriced!"*

Inevitably, during the weeks of work which precede a bazaar some of your group will become so enamored of their work and products that they wish to purchase them. The chairman hesitates to disappoint them, because they have personally been so involved with production. This poses a real dilemma, for at first glance, the old adage about a bird in the hand looks like sage advice. On the other hand, if there has been good publicity you have advertised to all and sundry that there will be quantities of merchandise to sell. It is hardly fair to lure the public to your benefit if they arrive to find all the prime merchandise has already been carefully picked over.

Here is where a sound piece of advice can be offered which all your workers can respect for its fairness. State it as your policy early in the game, and *stick to it*: Judging by the date of your affair, ascertain the latest date after which you will not have time to replace the merchandise, owing to the fact that workshop time is running out. Prior to that time, sell products which you can replace, and plow the money received back into supplies in order to make more merchandise. This will provide added financing to your strained budget and satisfy some of that urge to buy which was generated by your workers.

Oddly enough, you should listen to the inevitable criticism that certain products are overpriced. Sometimes you will feel quite slighted because you will know better than anyone else the amount of time and labor which was required to produce your product. But off-the-cuff reactions from people who are similar to your future customers may provide a clue to what is a reasonable or probable return to expect. Man-hours come cheap when labor is donated. This is why bazaars and benefits can survive in competition with well-run, cost-conscious stores. Remember, goodwill and free labor plus ingenuity are your only stocks-in-trade. Tiffany offers a famous name, gift packaging, charge accounts, and delivery service. Your offerings, although attractive, are not in the same category.

> *"We've Got to Have Someone Keep an Eye*
> *on the Money!"*

It always follows that the people who are most vocally interested in the profits of a bazaar are the same ones who seem to vanish when the work is to be done. They are likely to worry about someone making off with the profits or suggest with veiled comment that unnamed persons might be embezzling from the till. You will be well advised to have a financial committee from the start to which you can turn over profit as it accrues. Treat unwarranted inferences with a good sense of humor, and remember all you've learned about human nature. There are souls whose generosity will overwhelm you, and along with them come the inevitable Uriah Heeps. Assume honesty from all your co-workers, and they won't disappoint you.

> *"The Unbelievers" or "Worrywarts, Inc."*

At a recent church bazaar which involved an extremely enthusiastic congregation, one lady was bubbling over with excitement about the attractive products she had viewed on a visit to the bazaar workshops. During the week the ladies of the church had assembled (in the various church schoolrooms) their completed merchandise since it had to be stored away so that the schoolrooms could continue to be available for their regular purpose. One Sunday, an unthinking parishioner decided to go down and see for herself what all the fuss was about. Later she was heard to remark that she just couldn't see why there was such enthusiasm. She'd been down there to see the merchandise and found there was hardly anything available! It never occurred to her that such property could not be left around from week to week untended, to catch dust, and to create an attractive nuisance. The sour grapes gals are usually the ones who have a guilty conscience because they haven't put a hand to the wheel. A lot of us true believers got a good laugh out of this report, and it helped get us over some rough spots.

"I Wanted You to See This!" or
"Dust Catcher Products"

How do you tactfully dissuade one of your supporters who wants to diminish the quality of your products or merchandise with an idea that leaves you cold? You happen to feel that there are already too many "Johnny Planters" and itsy-cutesy dust catchers in the world, without your bazaar offering any more of the same. The answer is: You don't dissuade! You can set your sights high, and your overall offerings can be pretty special, but it is important to realize that there is a rather large market in our economy for just such dust catchers. What is one gal's poison is another's passport to happiness!

I will always remember a craft carnival at which a group of close friends of mine were busy setting up a display of their ceramics in a booth directly opposite mine. They displayed fine pieces along with unsold merchandise accumulated in the ceramic workshops they had attended during the year, and were donating their profits to the handicapped. When we all had finished setting up our exhibits, it was the custom to wander about the hall to admire each other's handiwork. A slender gray ceramic container

56

fashioned to resemble a piece of driftwood with a black squirrel resting on a limb caught my eye. I felt it would make a great container for a bouquet of pussy willows in the spring.

All my friends burst out in spontaneous laughter as I purchased the object, dirt cheap, for fifty cents. 'I think it's absolutely hysterical," said one of the women, wiping tears of laughter from her eyes. "All the way up here in the car we argued among us about what price we should put on these things in order to move them, and out of all the leftovers we had to offer, that's the thing that sold first."

"No one is fairer game for another crafter's merchandise than a fellow creator," I countered defensively, and proudly returned to my own display, completely happy with my purchase. That's what makes the world go 'round; there will be some at your bazaar who wouldn't know Tiffany's from the ten-cent store. In the ceramics area, I plainly had been guilty.

PLATE 18. Neat tables with wide aisles leave space for browsing.

IV

CHOOSING YOUR SITE AND MERCHANDISING SECRETS

Location

The layout of your bazaar will probably be dictated by your church, meeting rooms, clubhouse, or other available area. Don't hesitate to hire a hall or rent another church, however, if you have the membership and work force to think big. You will need space to display your wares if you want to make a large sum of money. If your membership is small, keep your bazaar area the same—something that you can reasonably handle—but go after excellence so that it will be for quality that you will be remembered. Make a point of this in your advertising so that your customers will expect the visit to your smaller benefit worth their while to make. The "We Try Harder" approach is a good one for a smaller organization.

Mini-Bazaars

There are some distinct advantages to a small bazaar, and many groups thrive on them. Mini-bazaars are very popular at my church when we are overloaded with other projects (yet the budget still has to be met). They are often conducted in a blocked-off area in a large auditorium or meeting room and offer a little bit of everything. Usually some other small program or entertainment is offered along with the sale.

One woman is assigned to each of ten or twelve tables, and she enlists her friends and neighbors to help her provide the

LAY-OUT FOR A MINI-BAZAAR

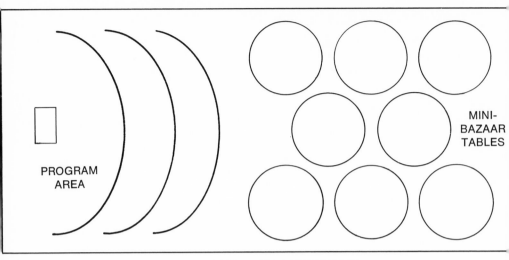

PROGRAM
AREA

MINI-
BAZAAR
TABLES

LARGE HALL OR AUDITORIUM

DELEGATION OF RESPONSIBILITY
FOR A LARGE BAZAAR:

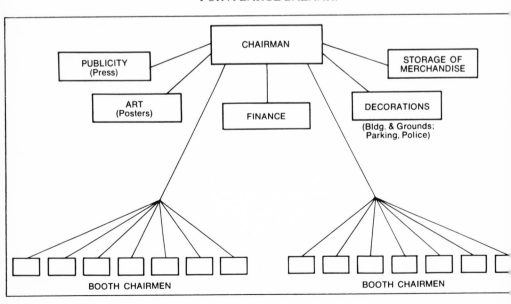

CHAIRMAN

PUBLICITY
(Press)

STORAGE OF
MERCHANDISE

ART
(Posters)

FINANCE

DECORATIONS

(Bldg. & Grounds;
Parking, Police)

BOOTH CHAIRMEN

BOOTH CHAIRMEN

merchandise they are to sell at them. She decorates and provides the theme for her own table, keeps track of her expenses, and, at bazaar day's end, deducts them from the profits realized. Each table chairman can do her own thing, and it can prove a very popular *modus operandi.*

The overall chairman lines up the table chairmen, handles the promotion and publicity, does general decoration, and dispenses ideas to those who need assistance. She may designate an overall theme to provide some organizational unity, but one of the interest factors of such a bazaar is in observing the various interpretations each table chairman will bring to her assignment.

Large Bazaars

The physical layout for a large bazaar should utilize proximity to specified areas. Food selling, restaurant, or coffee bar sales must be located near running water, electrical outlets, stoves, and general kitchen equipment. Leave uncluttered access to these areas for your workers, who will be tired quickly enough after serving customers through the many hours you are open for business. Block out clearly those areas where you do not want to see the public. Take nothing for granted, and spell out where seating will be available by the generous use of signs and arrows.

Stage areas are excellent for ongoing demonstrations or eye-catching displays, for example, a weaver at a loom, or a demonstrator at a potter's wheel, or a woman doing macramé. One or two of your most skilled workers can be featured doing more of the same in such a display area. If you cannot spare her on the day of the bazaar for such a viewing process, blown-up photographs of an artisan at work can effectively decorate the area around her displays.

Church schoolrooms are excellent for secondhand book sales because they are equipped with tables and chairs for browsers and children, your most active customers.

Merchandising Secrets

The food tables at a bazaar are seldom the largest money-makers, but they are important because they are a great drawing card for your customers. To begin with, most women who patronize your bazaar are doing so at the cost of leaving home and kitchen, so they are anxious to purchase something appetizing to take home. The key word in food-table operation is "appetizing"; it is my experience that if food is well presented and thought out, you will be sold out in two hours.

Easily transported items are most appealing, and finger foods that may be eaten on the spot are excellent sellers. Pie making is beginning to be a lost art, so assign any good pie makers to produce them if possible. After that is taken care of, a lot of know-how comes into focus. You cannot get too much fudge, brownies (good quality), cutout cookies, or cupcakes, and they may be sold by the unit or the half dozen. Time utilization on the part of your Food Committee is paramount here. For example, one food donor may spend the better part of an afternoon or morning baking you a cake which you can merchandise for $2. The *same time* expended by a donor who bakes up a triple recipe of good cutout butter cookies will net you three or four times the profit! Save old strawberry baskets (plastic), line them with a square piece of green nylon netting, and place nine large cutout cookies in each basket. These will sell quickly at 75 cents because they are eye-catching and transportable and will answer many home needs and requirements (school lunches, dessert, snacks for husband's den or office). Ten such baskets will triple the profit for the same time expended as that put in on a so-so cake. Colored sugars and a little time spent on decoration make these especially appealing at the Easter or Christmas holidays. Green or purple fruit or meat trays from the supermarket also make good cookie baskets for merchandising baked goods. If the food chairman will order floral, fruit, or leaf icing decorations through one of the baker's supply houses listed at the end of this book, she can make cupcakes and cakes of all sorts instantly appealing to the eye as they are delivered to the food table. Ask for white or chocolate icing, and *you* do the decorating. Violets, chicks, bunnies, wreaths, lilies—all are avail-

PLATE 19.   Coordinate books and products whenever possible.

The Jeremy Mouse Book by Patricia M. Scarry and illustrated by Hilary Knight is published by American Heritage Press.

able for the decoration of a plain cupcake, and it's the little touches that make all the difference.

An orange-juice can makes a wonderful container for a portion of jelly beans at Easter or hard candies at Christmas. Using Con-Tact adhesive papers around the body of the can, a floral pattern makes a lady's dress for a Mama Bunny, or striped red-and-white Con-Tact with a cutout black paper tie at the neck makes a Santa body, with striped shirting as his outfit. A face made from styrofoam balls fashioning either a bunny or a Santa (see Plate 20) and glued onto the top of the can finishes a very fetching product.

Inexpensive books also help make a combination product of great attraction. The 35-cent *I Like Christmas* book when sold with a toy or ornament makes an excellent child's Christmas gift, as does the dime-store *Gingerbread Man, The Spotted Puppy, The Calico Cat*, etc. Look over available dime-store books, and fashion your products to coordinate with them (Plate 19).

THE GINGERBREAD MAN ORNAMENT

Materials required: brown felt; small scraps of green and white felt; narrow red rickrack; red sequins; gold cord.

Cut two shapes of stiff brown felt in gingerbread man outline. Cut green jagged halo. Form thin gold hanger to attach. Glue together the two brown body shapes, inserting the green halo and gold cord at top. Decorate with white felt eyes, nose, mouth and bow tie; then glue narrow red rickrack around body and head surface, a separate tiny piece for head area. Use three sequins for buttons. Sell with *The Gingerbread Man* book.

Unusual recipes produce extra dollars if you have samples for demonstration or display. One extremely successful recipe which is authentic for Easter and interesting for spectators to learn about, is the Russian dessert known as the pashka, a unique dish made in a flowerpot. Such recipes may be mimeographed into a booklet and sold at a table, perhaps along with a taste sample offered on paper plates with plastic spoons (a little goes a long

PLATE 20.   Jelly beans from an orange-juice can and a gingerbread man—Christmas tree ornament and book make interesting bazaar gifts for children.

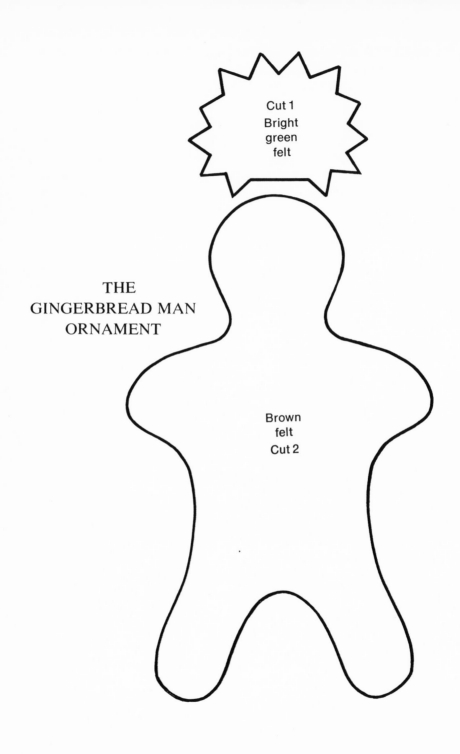

Cut 1
Bright
green
felt

THE
GINGERBREAD MAN
ORNAMENT

Brown
felt
Cut 2

way). Still another attraction at either Easter *or* Christmas is the Stained Glass Cookies (see Plate 16). Any distinctive recipe is an attraction at the food section of a good bazaar. Baked samples of the stand-up cookie patterns are appealing and spur people on to try duplication. I have used the elephant and bunny cookies in a bed of Easter grass, small Easter hats perched jauntily on their heads, as attention getters at Easter bazaars. They are also excellent when used with the Noah's Ark theme as well. The aforementioned and more offbeat recipes can be found in Chapter IX.

A STAND-UP COOKIE BUNNY

Materials required: cookie dough (the sugar cookie recipe in Chapter IX is recommended); cookie sheet; sharp knife; cardboard.

Trace pattern on cardboard and cut out. Then cut around pattern on cookie dough with sharp knife. The easiest way to cut out large pieces of dough, such as the body, is to roll dough initially on flat cookie sheet. Then remove spare pieces of dough for reuse. This eliminates lifting cookie parts before baking. Be sure to sharpen and accentuate notches with knife immediately upon removing cookies from oven, while hot and soft. Once the cookie hardens, it could crack. When thoroughly cool, stand up on bed of Easter grass. He's a real winner!

STAND-UP ELEPHANT COOKIE CENTERPIECE

Use any good sugar cookie recipe. Follow cookie pattern directions as listed for the Stand-Up Bunny Cookie. Display this young lady on a bed of paper flowers or Easter grass with a flower or paper hat behind her ear. She helps sell recipes. She is also great rainy-day fun for children or Scouts.

Slogans and up-to-date jargon help spur sales of bazaar objects. An empty large picture frame surrounded with stuffed dogs and puppies takes on new interest with a sign reading, "How much is that doggie in the window?" Pot holders sold from fish poles and objects sold from tree branches keep merchandise high and in full view of the public (see Plate 21).

PATTERN FOR A STAND-UP
COOKIE BUNNY

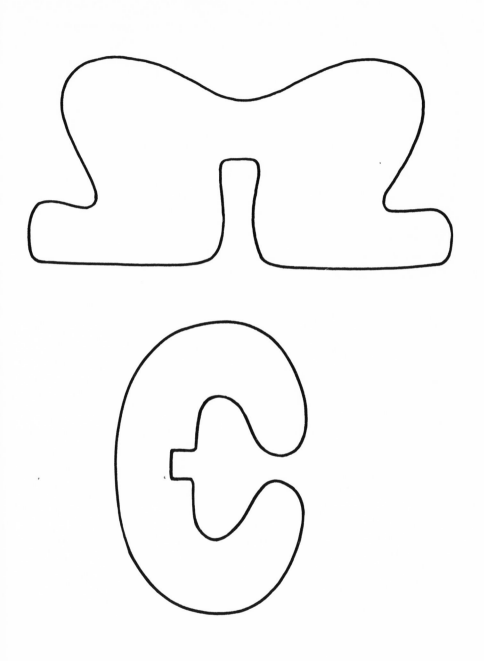

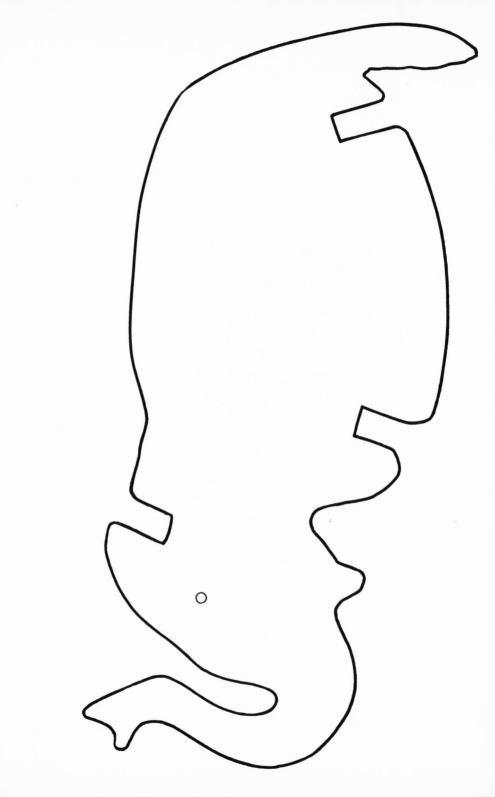

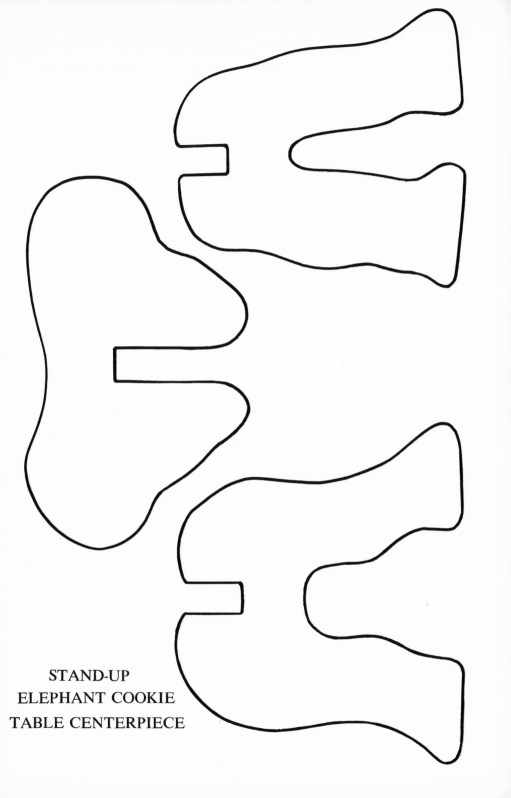

STAND-UP
ELEPHANT COOKIE
TABLE CENTERPIECE

PLATE 21. Spring products raised to new heights. Patterns for the pot holders displayed from branches here, are in Chapter 7.

Wide, uncluttered aisles and accessible tables are secrets of good merchandising. If the public cannot get to your tables, some good customers will leave without buying. Plain white butcher's paper with a neat border glued or scotch-taped to the table edges makes a good platform for effective selling. Neat, trim tables are more effective than bows and ribbons for decoration, since these tend to sag when put up beforehand. Keep extra merchandise below and behind tables for replenishment as the bazaar progresses. A good store does not put all its merchandise on the counter at once, and neither should the bazaar. Here the similarity ends. Remember that you do not furnish gift boxes, charge accounts, and delivery service, and take that into account in your pricing. Printed labels with the name of your organization can be ordered in advance and also serve as price tags which are neat and have an adhesive backing. In addition, posters help direct your public to booths of particular interest (see Plates 22 and 23).

A children's party table set with unbreakable Melamine ware by Betty Crocker for General Mills (see Chapter X), a poster setting the scene or event, is a wonderful way to raise a few extra dollars. This china comes in several patterns, the Peter Rabbit design being especially apropos for Easter, and Raggedy Ann and Andy or Red Riding Hood are great for Christmas. The table centerpiece might be nothing more elaborate than an open copy of the book. Extra merchandise can be stored under the table, and the place settings sell very quickly at a substantial profit to the bazaar. The service you offer is that the mail-order wait has been canceled for the customer, and he takes the package home. These make excellent baby presents and sell very quickly. A Sunday schoolroom table for tots makes an excellent setting for the sale. (See Plate 24.)

Extremely attractive as one enters the room of a bazaar is a giant mushroom, created out of an outdoor umbrella table swathed in old sheeting and stapled to the form. Red cardboard dots complete the mushroom cap. A rakish angle may be achieved by setting the umbrella at an angle. The table provides an excellent setting for viewing secondhand books, church-school

PLATE 22. Decorations of butterflies made from toothpaste boxes, snails from paper cups, and caterpillars from corrugated boxes.

PLATE 23.   Wide, clean, uncluttered aisles are essential to success.

chairs placed around the area for those who would browse. (See Plate 7A, page 31.)

Pompon yarn animals merchandised from nut cups are good sellers in the inexpensive product category. They can be fashioned from scraps of yarn which are donated, and Scout troops, teenagers, and Sunday school classes can contribute to your bazaar in this manner. Often these young designers are also a built-in buying public and come to your bazaar with the intention of purchasing the animal they helped fashion.

I have discovered that most people enjoy miniatures of one sort or another, and the perfect way to individualize a miniature is to fashion clothes to fit it. Advertise that at *your* bazaar, all your bunnies will wear hand-knit sweaters or stocking caps and sweaters at Christmas. These are quickly knitted by your handy knitters who will turn them out in quantity. They make unique and fetching toys which also *do* something, for the child recipient may dress and undress such stocking stuffers. What's more, they are great fun to make!

DIRECTIONS FOR MINIATURE CARDIGAN SWEATER

Starting at neck edge, cast on 40 sts. Work in ribbing, K 2, P 2, for three rows, making a buttonhole in second row of ribbing by putting yarn over and knitting two sts. together.

4th Row—Knit 3, purl across, knit last 3 sts.
Knit 3 sts. at beginning and end of every row for front border.

5th Row—K 3, increase in next two—K 2, increase in next 2, K 22 increase 2, K 2 increase 2, K 3.

6th Row—K 3, purl across, ending K 3.

7th Row—K 4, increase 2, K 4, increase 2, K 24 increase 2, K 4 increase 2, K 4.

8th Row—K 3, purl across, ending K 3.

9th Row—K 5, increase 2, K 6, increase 2, K 26, increase 2, K 6 increase 2, K 5.

76

PLATE 24.   Who could resist wares sold under a poster such as this?

10th Row—K 3, purl, K 3.

11th Row—K 6, increase 2, K 8, increase 2, K 28, increase 2, K 8, increase 2, K 6.

12th Row—K 3, purl, K 3.

13th Row—K 7, increase 2, K 10, increase 2, K 30, increase 2, K 10, increase 2, K 7.

14th Row—K 3, purl, K 3.

15th Row—K 8, increase 2, K 12, increase 2, K 32, increase 2, K 12, increase 2, K 8.

16th Row—K 3, purl, K 3.

17th Row—K 10, place next 16 on stitch holder for sleeve. K 36 on same needle as first 10, then put next 16 on another stitch holder for other sleeve, and knit last 10 on same needle. You should now have 56 sts. on needle. Continue 1 row Knit, 1 row Purl, keeping 3 border sts. in Knit for 3 rows, then knit all rows for 3 rows for border, and cast off all sts.

For sleeve—pick up 16 sts. and work 1 row Knit and 1 row Purl for four rows, then 3 rows ribbing, K 2, P 2, for 3 rows. Cast off. Pick up other 16 sts. from holder and work same as first sleeve. Sew up under arm seam. Sew on small button opposite side of buttonhole.

DIRECTIONS FOR TINY STOCKING CAP TO GO WITH MINIATURE SWEATER

Cast on 12 sts.

Garter stitch for next 5 rows.

Knit, decreasing at beginning and end of next row (every 4th row thereafter at beginning and end of each row, decrease 1 stitch).

Do this four times, or 16 rows.

Bind off. Sew up sides. Make a pompon tassel, leaving enough yarn to sew it on.

DIRECTIONS FOR TINY STRAIGHT CAP
TO GO WITH MINIATURE SWEATER

Cast on 12 sts.

Work garter stitch for 3 rows (knitting every row).

Work K 1, P 1, for 6 rows.

Now you are decreasing. K 2 together 6 times, over the 12 sts. Break yarn—take needle and draw through 6 sts., pulling very tight.

In several examples in this book I refer to the modern idea of selling by slogan. The American buying public is especially receptive to this technique. It will also serve you well at your bazaar.

The Psychedelic Centipede is a case in point (see p. 93, Chapter VI). Give your bazaar divisions and products catchy names to attract the public. One prime example of slogan merchandising is the Water Weenie by Wham-O. This product is simply a balloon filled with water. How much more exciting to describe and merchandise is the Water Weenie. Give your products humorous, fanciful, imaginative, mind-stretching names, and put them on your posters and in your ads. If you need a gimmick to sell the public, make it a *great gimmick.*

V

PROMOTION: "IT PAYS TO ADVERTISE"

I recently attended an institutional open house which was scheduled for Palm Sunday. The object of the promotion was to interest and acquaint local doctors with the opening of a large health center, and much expense was entailed in organizing the holiday help, ordering and serving the food and liquor, mailing out printed invitations, and staffing the area to handle the expected crowds. Only one thing turned out to be missing—the expected medical guests. So much time and energy and effort had gone into scheduling the event that nobody had inquired into the holiday habits of the doctors whom they wished to interest. The simplest investigation would have shown that doctors are jealous of their weekend time and that holidays are about the least effective time to try to interest them in any outside medical activity. No one had taken the time to find this out, so the open house turned out to be an exercise in futility.

Dates and timing are absolutely essential considerations when you are planning for your bazaar, so pick the date carefully and make some inquiry beforehand. School and church calendars and locally obtainable information are good barometers of possible conflict. We have already considered what holiday seasons will work under certain conditions, and dates are important also if you want children to attend your function, particularly if husbands are involved or are potential buyers, for it is obvious that if children are in school, they cannot be considered important customers.

Even more important than the date is your advertising. Bear this in mind when you are selecting your chairman of publicity, for this appointment is not one for the timid. The good publicity chairman is innovative, has know-how, respects deadlines, and does things with a flair. Her skills are crucial. This is one job where the gal who puts things off and can't get excited doesn't belong. Her knowledge and excitement are diffused through personal contacts and written copy, and her follow-through is essential. Customers don't buy until you get them into the store, it's just that simple.

Most radio stations will plug your date and event if they receive your typed material (copy) at least two weeks in advance. The morning shows on local radio and TV stations are generally cooperative. I am informed that over and over radio stations have received promotional copy from one group or another who forget to include such an obvious bit of information as the *date!*

Newspapers have deadlines, and the alert publicity chairman sends out advance write-ups describing the date of the bazaar and interesting descriptions of the products and services you will have to offer. If the chairman calls the club news editor of the local paper a few weeks in advance, she may very well cooperate and send out a photographer to give you some advance publicity. If the thoroughness of your publicity chairman includes a statement of the reasons behind your fund raising, the news media will often lend valuable assistance in getting your message across. Address your communications to the Club News Editor, double space your *typewritten* message, and inscribe at the top: FOR IMMEDIATE RELEASE. At the end of your communiqué, list your name, address, and telephone number so that you may be reached instantly if further information is desired.

Poster up the town with *readable*, uncluttered advertisements, the printing large and unencumbered. Send a flyer to the nearby schools to be posted, for teachers will want to support you, too, especially if lunch-hour fare is offered. Mimeograph a letter beginning "Dear ———," and describe the profusion of products and services you will be offering, including the date and hours of the event. Leave these in a conspicuous place for your membership to pick up in quantity so they can mail them to their friends. They won't do it if they must list all the merchandise

81

personally, *but they will if you make it painless.* Leave nothing to chance!

I once received a folded brown paper bag in the mail, carefully addressed and properly stamped, and as I unfolded the length of it, I was greeted with the following legend, mimeographed on a small stapled sheet of paper:

IS THIS YOUR BAG?
CHRISTMAS FAIR
SPONSORED BY
THE
GUILD FOR CHRISTIAN SERVICE
ST. ANDREWS EPISCOPAL CHURCH, SCARSDALE, N.Y.
BOOTHS & GIFTS FOR ALL AGES
DATES:_____
HOURS:_____

They did a brisk business at that bazaar, because someone had a flair!

Below is a sample promotion letter which can be mailed to all your supporters before your bazaar. Such a letter can be highly effective in publicity value.

Spring, 1973

Dear _____,

Please save Saturday, March _____, for a marvelously cheerful spring outing. The women of the Greenville Community Reformed Church, Ardsley Road and Central Avenue, Scarsdale, are having a sparkling Easter bazaar with fresh, perky merchandise guaranteed to lift your spirits and take you right out of the winter doldrums. We'll have favors for your Easter table, Easter egg trees, violet topiaries, bunnies in hand-knit sweaters and caps, panoramic, scene-decorated eggs for mantel and end tables, summer fruits with luscious Easter scenes within, table settings, children's bunny ware, traditional Russian pashka dessert (how to make it, with free sampling provided), all manner of gourmet delights, including special Easter breads for the Big Morning, Easter baskets made to order for shut-ins, teen-

82

agers, and children. Look for real treasures in secondhand hats and jewelry. Fishpond, ladybug toys, mobiles, books for children and adults (whole sets of *Raggedy Ann, Nancy Drew, Bobbsey Twins,* etc.).

Lift your spirits and welcome the Lenten season with us. Breakfast coffee and doughnuts, luncheon, and snacks will be served. Yes, prices are down to earth, too. We'd like your goodwill, as well as your good wishes, as we work to diminish the mortgage on this beautiful church.

Cordially,

P.S. Yes, we'll have Mushroom Corners or "Rummage for Everyone," and a treasure trove of donated objects with real interest!

SAVE THE DAY!

RABBIT POSTER

Materials required: white poster board; orange construction paper; shirt cardboard; scotch tape.

Here is a suggested pattern for a promotional sign advertising an Easter bazaar. Carrot for bunny, plus standard, is included. The rabbit is made of strong white poster board. The carrot is made of orange construction paper, scotch-taped to the rabbit's mouth and paw. Cut the standard from shirt cardboard and glue to the back side of the rabbit.

In your advertising and promotion be sure to capitalize on the fun in anticipating an event. It is well recognized that one of the greater joys of attending a function is the looking forward to it: counting the days, marking off the weeks—*real* anticipation! Build up your public in a breathless way to the goodies that will be theirs for the asking when they plan to attend your celebration.

Sometimes curiosity and mystery may be involved in your anticipatory advertising. Choose one popular aspect of the bazaar, blow it up to larger-than-life dimensions in your press and poster releases. Plug your Baby-Care Booth with posters and signs

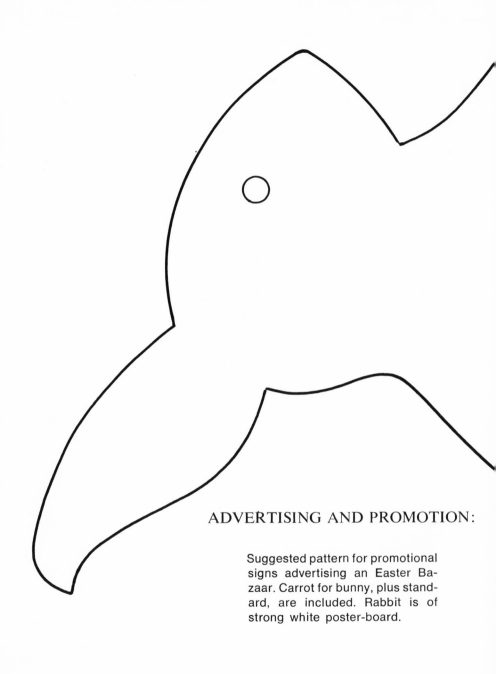

ADVERTISING AND PROMOTION:

Suggested pattern for promotional signs advertising an Easter Bazaar. Carrot for bunny, plus standard, are included. Rabbit is of strong white poster-board.

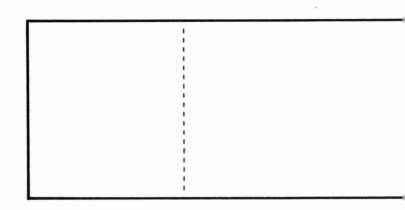

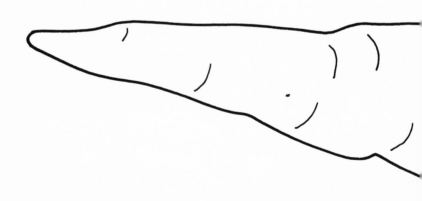

Carrot is made of orange construction paper, scotch-taped to
mouth and paw of rabbit.

Cut standard out of shirt cardboard and glue to backside of
rabbit.

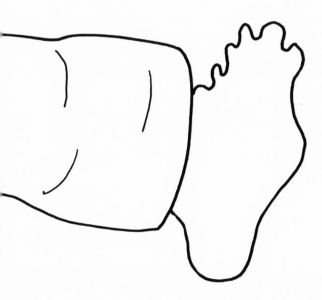

reading "Bazaar Babies Get Better Billing at the the St. Andrews Christmas Bazaar." Or "Mystery Merchandise at St. Andrews in Millwood! Come and Enjoy Madcap Mayhem at Our Merry Christmas Bazaar!" Today your promotion might read:

Santa Is a Scorpio! at St. Cecilia's on Saturday. Meet Your Astrologer at Our Bazaar in the Month of Sagittarius (December 5 to all you armchair celestial students). Let the Stars Guide You — to Our Re-creation of the Greatest Star of All: the Star of Bethlehem. We'll have:

1. Starry-eyed kids
2. Tree-top stars
3. Star 'n' crescent cookies
4. Stars in our chicken soup
5. Peppermint stars
6. Sno-flake stars
7. *Star*tlingly beautiful products to sell

Start right now to get ready for December 5!

A large sign that will endure blowing in the wind may be fashioned from an old white sheet, painted in waterproof lettering and strung between two trees on the premises. It should be nailed to and reinforced by two flat two-by-fours pushed into the ground at equal distances, to lend it support in the case of strong winds.

VI

COMMON BAZAAR PITFALLS
(TECHNICAL, FINANCIAL, PERSONAL)

There are personal, technical, and financial ground rules for the proper functioning of a modern-day bazaar.

The chairman of a bazaar should be able to envision the forest, as well as the trees, for it is she who must pull it all together. If she is able to delegate responsibility, she will not lose sight of her forest. I see the chairman's role as that of enthusiast and invigorator. Her spirit and goals can be positive and infectious, because in her mind's eye she sees the need for the result of all that cumulative labor. I do not see important fund raising as "female busywork." On reading Dr. Karl Menninger's famous *Criteria for Emotional Maturity* I was struck by the similarities of values between such a standard and the achievements of a bazaar committee working with willing hands toward a common goal. Among other factors Dr. Menninger lists his criteria as: "Having the ability to deal constructively with reality; having the capacity to relate to other people in a consistent manner with mutual satisfaction and helpfulness" and, finally, "having the capacity to sublimate, to direct one's hostile energy into creative and constructive outlets."* I can only comment—what else is a bazaar unless it is people exemplifying all these things?

Another important function of the chairman is to prevent the duplication of labor. Without involving herself in all the minutiae of detail, she will have sufficient grasp of the functions of her various committees to prevent time-consuming overlapping of

* From the writings of Dr. Karl Menninger. Used by special permission of his son, Phillip Menninger.

effort. The simple surveillance of who is doing what need not result in an officious attitude.

Some technical aspects of bazaar giving are involved in checking out the health and fire regulations for the buildings your group will occupy. Is there a limit to the number of people permitted in the building? A quick call to the local fire marshal will answer all such questions.

With regard to entertainment other than that of selling merchandise at booths and counters, if any aspect of your program is professional, have a firm contract to guard you against last-minute substitutions or failure to appear.

We have previously discussed how money should be handled at large and small bazaars, but there are still the matters of tax and insurance to consider. With regard to the collection of taxes, consult the local revenue office or your state or local tax department. For your own information as well, keep accurate records of income and expenses for your project.

Make sure that you have appropriate liability coverage. Since, for a one-day bazaar, large amounts of money are collected on the premises, it may be wise to have one-day insurance coverage as a guard against robbery, especially of an advertised event.

This chapter and many subjects covered herein should prove especially helpful to those working with children in scouting or church school or with the physically handicapped, as well as to the chairman of a bazaar (or any fund-raising fair for that matter). *A successful bazaar provides many inexpensive items for children to buy.* I believe the best way to flounder in a bazaar project is to price the merchandise too high, and many a group has had to learn this lesson the hard way. The real trick is to find an attractive, inexpensive-to-duplicate product with a catchy name that can be made in quantity at very little cost. Then volume makes it a secure seller. A good bazaar ought to offer two or three such items, distributed strategically at various booths to draw the public and highly visible to children. Usually such products are small (because inexpensive) and make excellent stocking stuffers at Christmas or basket fillers at Easter; therefore, the adult public will be drawn to these products, too. The most

PLATE 25. The Psychedelic Centipede wins the hearts of everyone who sees him. Sells effectively when displayed on a manzanita branch.

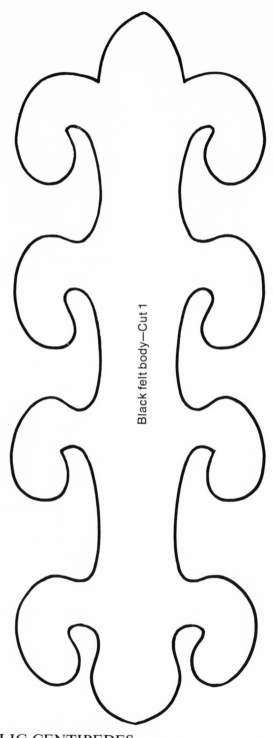

Black felt body—Cut 1

PSYCHEDELIC CENTIPEDES

successful object of this sort that I have ever encountered is the Psychedelic Centipede! He was featured at a spring bazaar, and we opened up our selling day with about 400 of him in hand (the bazaar followed a school spring vacation period. Numerous teen-agers had dropped in to work at the workshops prior to the bazaar, and this was a product they could turn out with very little instruction). It was a simple procedure involving assemblage, gluing, and cutting. We sold out in about an hour selling them at 50 cents apiece, and made a quick, heady profit. (See Plate 25.)

PSYCHEDELIC CENTIPEDE OR THAT CRAZY CATERPILLAR

Materials required: *large* white ball fringe; various additional colors of small ball fringe; paper flower centers (stamens) for antennae; black felt; scraps of red felt; bright-colored thick package-wrapping yarn by Hallmark or Norcross.

Large white ball forms the head. Arrange a pleasing-to-the-eye sequence of 12 balls cut from ball fringe, glueing each to the preceding one, forming a line; then attach this body to white head. Glue entire body to felt underside. When dry, it is quite flexible. Cut off 1½-inch piece of thick yarn for tail, and glue it to last ball in body sequence.

Cut underpinning of caterpillar from black felt according to pattern:

PING AND PONG, THE PANDA PUPPET TWINS

Panda puppets are another item that fulfills many different kinds of requirements. They have been used successfully when working with the physically handicapped, who may be given the presewn black puppet shape to decorate with the fat panda belly (an all-white ball from ball fringe) and the already decorated pompon face (sold by the yard as ball fringe also). To assemble the finished puppet is the satisfaction derived.

Materials required: black felt; white chenille ball fringe; ball fringe with red and black face (available through Cosmo Trims, Cosmo Products, Inc., 27 West Twenty-third Street, New York, New York), which has been woven into the white ball with wool.

93

PLATE 26.   Panda Puppets and a wide-eyed ladybug pin.

PING & PONG THE PANDA PUPPET TWINS

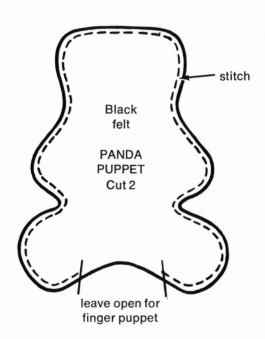

stitch

Black
felt

PANDA
PUPPET
Cut 2

leave open for
finger puppet

PLATE 27. New plastic fabrics open up toy possibilities extremely realistic in appearance. A three-inch-wide free-form wavy line is the only pattern needed for a squishy snake filled with birdseed.

PLATE 28.   Recycling a container which reflects the designing skill of a modern manufacturer can also help you originate new bazaar products. Utilize it for your own ends.

PLATE 29.   Stylish,   budget-priced   volume   sellers   for   a   modern bazaar. Shown, left to right, Reggie Reindeer, a Psychedelic Centipede and Lily Ladybug.

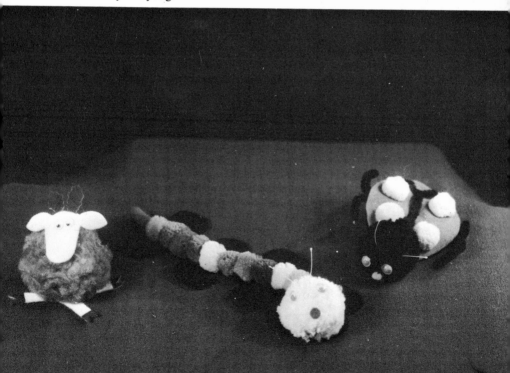

A ladybug product is interesting to children and is the same in principle as the Psychedelic Centipede; it is large enough to be mounted on a glued pin backing (available at all hobby shops) so that it may be worn on hats, jeans, or lapels. Reggie Reindeer is another good brisk-selling Christmas item. A cute, small toy accessory of this sort, mounted on a jewelry pin backing, may be worked out to fit almost any theme for a bazaar, whether chick, worm, strawberry, or whatever one desires; they will sell at a good profit for 50 cents.

Failure to provide inexpensive items is a gross oversight at a good bazaar. It is also wise to offer products suitable to the tastes of a small boy since women and little girls cannot afford to overlook the young male customer. Alligators, frogs, and snakes, squishy objects filled with birdseed, bug-jug containers, collect-a-zoo (products all merchandised from empty Jet-Dry water-softening baskets originally containing soap for dishwashers) are all of a kind to appeal to young boys or to grandmothers who "know" them. Place a plastic bug (wired),* along with the mimeographed legend of how to care for and keep a live one, on some of these baskets, and little boys will quickly spend a quarter. The whole Mattel line (dime store) of zoo animals (those which can fit inside the tiny baskets) may be offered in a collect-a-zoo display. Many small fry will purchase the entire set. These same baskets, a bright red bird on the handle, make suet holders for bird lovers; sprayed gold, they make lovely bird-cage ornaments for Christmas, the tiny red bird inside the cage, hung from a gilt cord hanger; lined with pastel silk and decorated, they make an attractive ring holder for the windowsill above milady's kitchen sink. Many thousands of dollars went into the final design and manufacture of this lovely little basket, and it's yours for the recycling. (See Plates 27 and 28.)

LILY LADYBUG (PLATE 29)

Materials required: red pile; black felt; black ball fringe in

* The Pink Sleigh Catalog.

large size; yellow pipe-cleaners; jewelry pin backing (available from hobby shops); scraps of red felt; rolling eyes.

Cut 2 red pile oval overbodies; glue on yellow felt dots cut with a paper punch. Glue this in turn onto black felt underbody; add head of large ball fringe, with rolling eyes and red felt mouth. Glue on bent pipe-cleaner antennae. Attach pin to underside for child's novelty.

REGGIE REINDEER (PLATE 29)

Materials required: white felt; black felt scraps; red ball fringe in large size; green felt scraps.

Using the largest red ball fringe obtainable, or a homemade pompon yarn ball such as those used in pompon animals, cut felt reindeer face (white), body and legs (also white) to fashion the reindeer. Add rolling eyes, green felt holly leaf ears (or horns), and black felt paws. Mount a pin on the felt underside, and put one on all your salespeople. Sells well as a pin or silly stocking stuffer during the holidays.

INEXPENSIVE FELT BAZAAR PINS
TO MAKE FOR CHILDREN

FLIPPIE FROG:

Materials required: lime green felt; scraps of shocking pink, red, and light blue felt; rolling eyes; jewelry pin backing.

Glue two pieces of lime green felt, cut in the shape of the frog, together. Glue on red mouth and shocking pink bowtie. Glue on rolling eyes. Sew pin on back surface.

CASPER GHOST:

Materials required: heavy black felt; white felt; pin backing.

Cut black felt ghost shape as shown in pattern. Cut white felt ghost shape and glue on top of larger black shape. Glue on black eyes and mouth. The eyes may be punched out with a paper punch. Sew pin to underside.

PATTERNS FOR LILY LADYBUG
AND REGGIE REINDEER

Ladybug; cut 2 red pile oval over-bodies—glue on yellow felt dots cut with paper punch. Glue this in turn onto black felt underbody; add head of black large size ball fringe, with rolling eyes and red felt mouth. Glue on bent pipe cleaner antennae. Attach pin to underside for child's novelty.

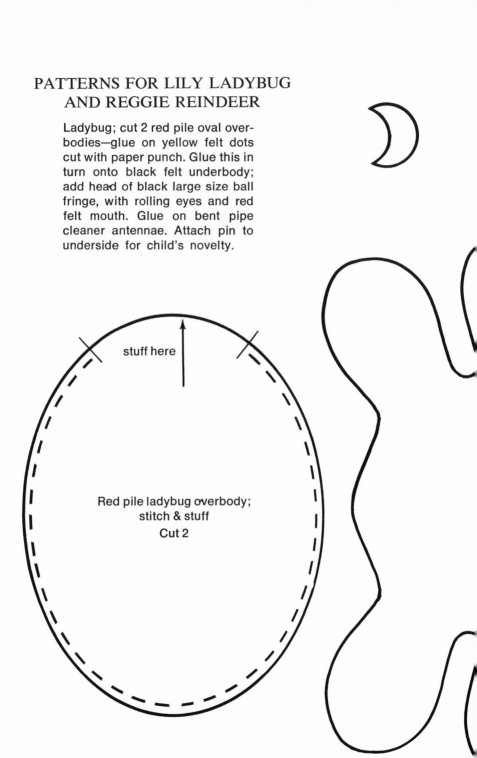

stuff here

Red pile ladybug overbody;
stitch & stuff
Cut 2

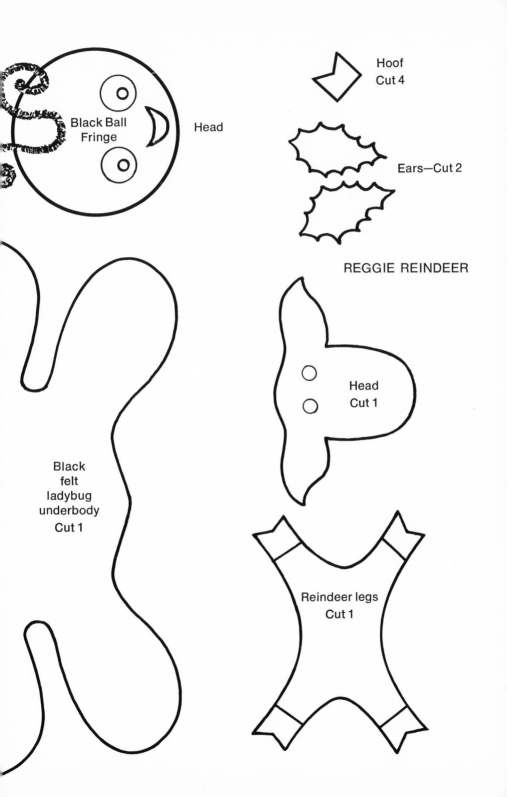

Black Ball
Fringe

Head

Hoof
Cut 4

Ears—Cut 2

REGGIE REINDEER

Head
Cut 1

Black
felt
ladybug
underbody
Cut 1

Reindeer legs
Cut 1

INEXPENSIVE FELT BAZAAR PINS TO MAKE
FOR CHILDREN

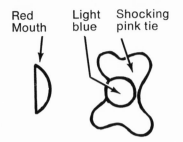

Red
Mouth

Light
blue

Shocking
pink tie

FLIPPIE FROG

Cut 2
Lime green
felt

Glue two pieces of lime green
(cut in frog shape) together. S
pin on back surface.

CASPER GHOST

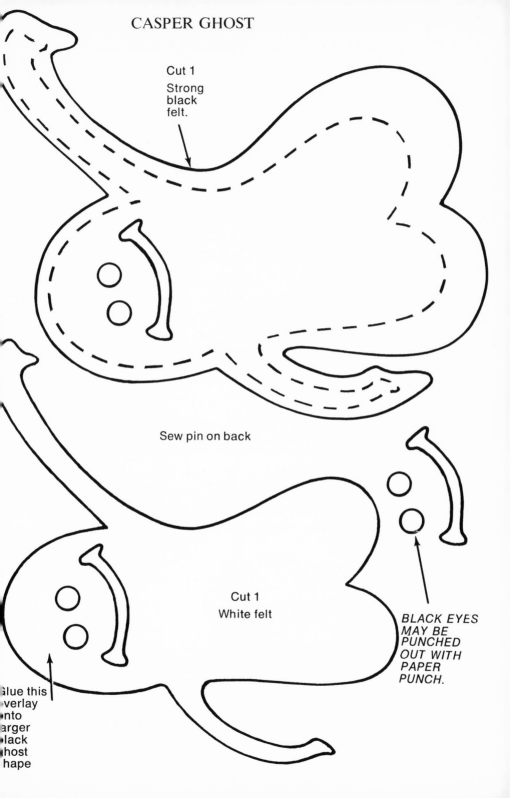

Cut 1
Strong black felt.

Sew pin on back

Cut 1
White felt

BLACK EYES MAY BE PUNCHED OUT WITH PAPER PUNCH.

Glue this overlay onto arger black ghost hape

PLATE 30. A peck of mice.

The tiny, inexpensive mouse is a constant strong seller, whether sold as a pincushion or as a toy. He is particularly attractive merchandised from a Christmas Santa red felt boot or from a peck fruit basket, tail hanging out. For the pincushion, the eyes made of black sequins, do not have to be sewn on, but are secured in place with a white or colored pin dot; a black pin dot serves as the nose. Mice are made from scrap fabrics and are as gay as the fabric. At Christmas, he is the "Christmas Mouse," and no respectable house should be without one. Tiny wreaths from the Pink Sleigh add the finishing touch about his neck. Or give him a tiny "Grandma Stover" champagne bottle.* A band of mice following a pied piper doll is a smashing display group on a Christmas bazaar table, Christmas village decorations completing the setting.

Your costs for this product can be almost nothing if you use up scraps of fabric or use decorator's sample swatches, which they are generally willing to give away once patterns are outdated or obsolete.

Cut two mouse body pieces and one bottom piece, then two mouse ears from matching or contrasting colors of felt. Starting at nose end, right sides together, sew sides to bottom. Stitch across top, sewing down braided yarn tail at end. Turn mouse right side out, pulling through slit in the bottom. Stuff with nylon fiber fill and slip-stitch shut (See Plate 30).

Sometimes a basically sound product misses in eye appeal because the proper attention to finishing detail was not observed. The addition of one little touch can make all the difference. The calico dog and cat, Plate 31, were always sold with a tiny bell around the neck, and it was the finishing touch that added so much appeal to the product. Fresh ribbon, cellophane, or Baggies to keep products perky and fresh—all pay off at the cash receipts counter. Take the trouble to contact a sachet or cosmetics manufacturer for sample perfume or sachet packets to sell with a toy

* Grandma Stover's Miniatures, found in novelty and party shops.

MINI-MICE

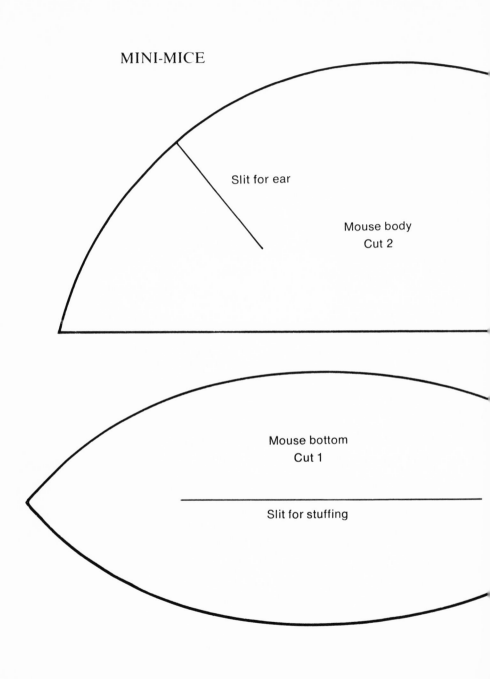

Slit for ear

Mouse body
Cut 2

Mouse bottom
Cut 1

Slit for stuffing

Eyes are black sequins held on with pin dots. Black pin nose.

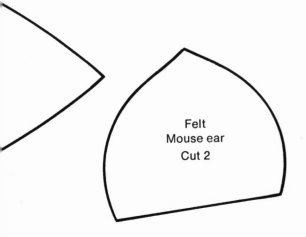

Felt
Mouse ear
Cut 2

PLATE 32. Plant cuttings in miniature containers sell well year round.

PLATE 33. There's always a bargain at the jewelry table.

PLATE 31. The gingham dog, calico cat, and a child's apron with toy insert in pocket.

PLATE 34.   A rag doll with her clutch ball
toys.

stuffed skunk. By saving the clear, plastic bags which come
around hosiery bought by the box, see-through merchandising
can be used on your flat products which store well until your sale,
and products are kept fresh and clean. Banks and other stores
frequently give away small fold-up plastic rain hats which can
be used to accompany soft toy ducks or any product associated
with raindrops.

110

A few plants generally sell well if you do not want to get into a large plant display. In the spring, merchandise a dainty plant such as baby tears from bright small egg cups. An appeal for these among your membership generally produces some interesting shapes and sizes of these in odd numbers; start the plants well in advance of your bazaar from a single $2 plant, and subdivided into the small containers, this makes a good profit. Single decorative tea cups in saucers (odd handouts from a congregation) can also be planted in this way to make a salable item. African violet cuttings or begonia cuttings are excellent for this. (See Plate 32.)

Secondhand jewelry is also always a brisk business getter, and its display is paramount to the success of the table. Better pieces are shown to advantage on black or navy velvet, as a jeweler would do. Wide spacing of the area where customers will be milling enables them to look carefully as they are choosing and deciding. A jewelry table should never be placed in a crowded, congested area.

The large clutch ball shown in Plate 34 did not sell because it was too large for a ball toy and had not been adequately thought through by its designer. However, we finally sold them all at succeeding bazaars because someone thought up the label "TV Pillows," and a useful idea for an oversized product was born, with a real purpose behind it. The smaller clutch ball is always a brisk seller for babies and young children. They are most appealing when made up in the new patterned terry cloth combined with a solid color, and cut-up stockings make economical, washable stuffing for these balls.

Signs depicting the use of the product you are selling helps the prospective buyer see herself using it. Do not leave it up to the customer to figure out a use for your offerings. Much of the public has little or no imagination, and that's where *you* come in.

PLATE 35. Noah's Ark, a smashing bazaar attention getter, made from pink pillow cases. Noah's Ark kits may be purchased from a supplier (see Chapter X).

VII

PERKY PRODUCTS

Today's women's magazines are a tremendous source of aid and assistance to the woman running a bazaar. Generally, if one knows well in advance that a money-raising function is on the calendar, a systematic perusal, over a few months' time, of the magazines at your disposal can be an invaluable aid in the development of merchandise that is up to date and fashionable. If a flexibility of mind is brought to the situation, you will find these periodicals helpful in the choice of a theme for your project; in addition, they will offer know-how on ideas for products to make which, with a little imagination on *your* part, can be altered or changed or reemphasized so as to serve your particularly specialized purposes.

An overall theme such as "Noah's Ark," "An African Safari," "The Saturday Circus," or "Beatrix Potter Times" opens wide the vistas of the animal world and all the wealth of concepts and ideas which develop from them. Books, products, pony rides, stuffed animals, caricatures, posters—all lend themselves to the Disney-Dolittle concept of animal life, and they are surefire themes because every human being responds to animals.

The whole world is currently entranced with the cuddly, fetching panda bears recently sent from China to the United States. We expect to feature the panda at our next Christmas bazaar, for he comes from snowy climes, and his rich black and white coloring will be stunning against the reds and greens of Christmas. The koala bear is another animal which captivates both young and old. To develop this theme, we will turn to *Woman's Day* magazine, which offers a brochure of *Special Offers of Things to*

PLATE 36.   Just between us caterpillars. . . .

PLATE 37.   Goofy guys but great bazaar buys!

Make and Do on almost any topic, projects they have featured dating back to 1962. The brochure may be obtained by writing to *Woman's Day*, P.O. Box 1000, Greenwich, Conneticut 06830. Looking for material on bears, a theme can gradually develop which suggests innumerable possibilities: a Teddy Bear's Christmas; the Three Bears Fair; Koala Bear's Kristmas; (Panda Posters; Smoky Bear Products; Yogi Bear; Honey and Honey Products; Circuses and Performing Bears.) I know immediately that our food bar will be called the Honey Pot, and the children's game area will be Jellystone Park. Before we know it, perky products emerge and fall into line. The *Woman's Day* brochure gave several "bear" products to use.

Our last spring bazaar took its character from the caterpillar, and lime green smily caterpillars hung from the ceiling, cut from connecting circles of corrugated paper, painted and cut into long green lengths.* We featured three separate sizes and concepts of caterpillars in the products we offered for sale. The largest of these was the Draft Dodger, a yard-long stuffed animal which serves a true purpose in keeping drafts from an outside door when stretched out along the floor. But he proved so winning to teen-agers that we sold many just for bed toys and room decorations (see Plate 36). I found the pattern for him tucked away in the Special Projects Christmas Issue of *Family Circle* magazine of 1971 (see Chapter X).

Next came an educational toy product, the Worrisome Worm, made from a series of circles (twelve in all) which connect to each other with dressmaker snaps, so that a child can assemble and reassemble the creature while learning graduated sizes (see Plate 37).

And last, but not least, came the small Psychedelic Centipede described earlier.

THE WORRISOME WORM

Materials required: patterned cotton color-coordinated with

* See Wind Swingers, Bazaar Decorations, Easter Tips: Chapter X; also Plates 22-23 Chapter IV.

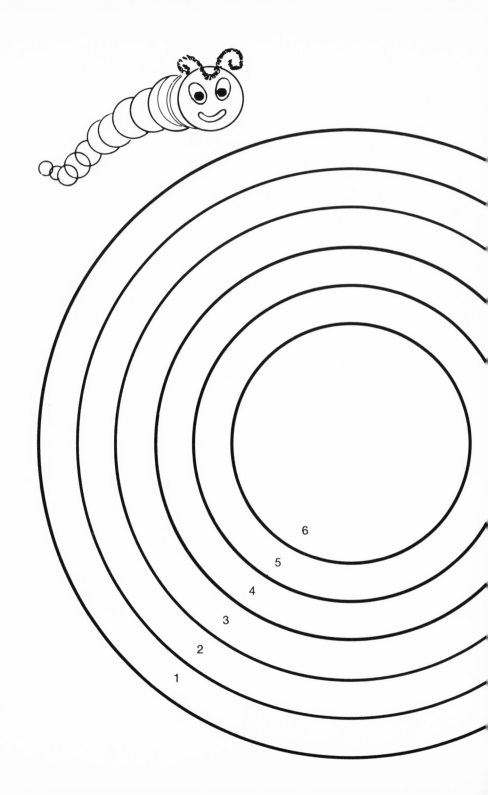

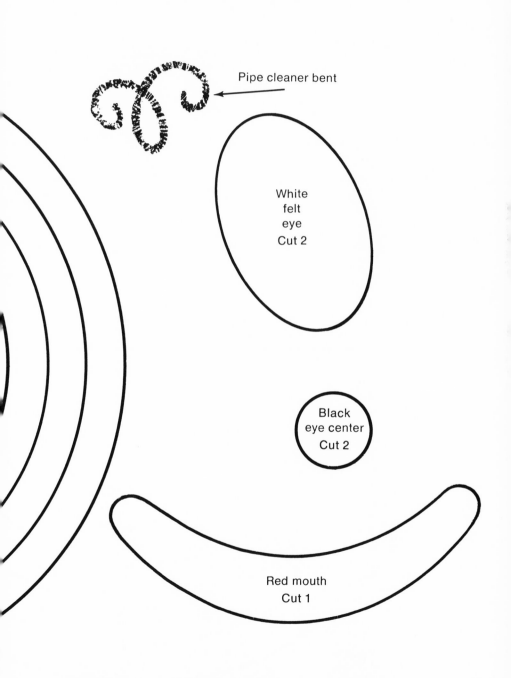

Pipe cleaner bent

White
felt
eye
Cut 2

Black
eye center
Cut 2

Red mouth
Cut 1

solid cotton; 1 large pipe cleaner, same color; 11 large upholstery snaps; kapok stuffing; scraps of red, white and black felt.

Trace onto cardboard or sandpaper patterns of 6 graduated circles. Lay the six circles on patterned, then solid fabric, folded into 2 layers. Cut 2 of each circle size in both fabrics. Sew together 1 patterned circle and 1 solid circle, right sides together. Turn and stuff firmly. Repeat for remaining 11 circles. Twelve circles constitute one worm, two of each of the six sizes. Sew large snaps in center of all 12 circles, head circle (largest) having only one snap on back side (plain side will have face). Put face on front of largest circle (glue), stitch down bent pipe-cleaner antennae by hand. Worm will be about ¾ yard long.

PLATE 38.   Christmas ornaments and products from a Calico Christmas.

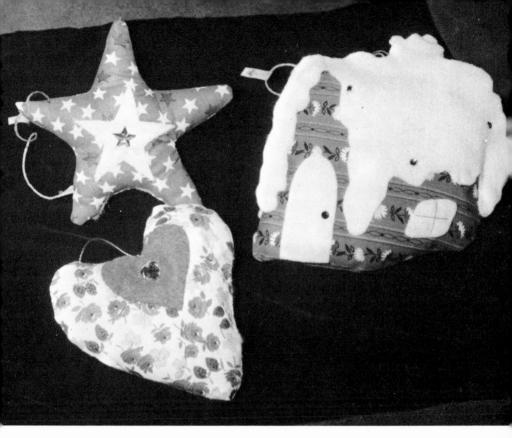

PLATE 39.   Even the treetop star is of calico.

Stocking stuffers of animal shapes, sold from paint-mixing cardboard buckets are a natural for blending in with all the themes described. They are also fascinating tree ornaments if a hanger is attached. Some of the most winning are included here: Denny Dinosaur, Snoopy Snail, Ollie Octopus, Ronnie Rabbit, Toby Tiger—all fill the bill! And let's not forget the red plaid train!

In addition, all these products can be introduced similarly at A Calico Christmas or A Country Christmas. A whole line of Christmas ornaments can be fashioned of calico, and the biggest seller is the red-striped cotton candy cane! Customers are overjoyed to find a candy cane for their tree which hasn't any calories! (See Plates 38 and 39.)

119

DENNY DINOSAUR:

Materials required: bright green poplin for body; fiberfill stuffing; crystal glass button eyes.

SNOOPY SNAIL:

Materials required: narrow black rickrack; small black button for eye; scraps of yellow yarn; brown/black cotton print fabric for body; fiberfill stuffing.

OLLIE OCTOPUS:

Materials required: patterned fabric in a vibrant color for body; scraps of white and black felt; braided yarn for tentacles in an appropriate color to match the material used; fiberfill stuffing. Stuff at bottom and hand sew tentacles when you stitch shut.

RONNIE RABBIT:

Materials required: blue and white checked cotton fabric; scraps of white and pink felt; scraps of black yarn; fiberfill stuffing.

TOBY TIGER:

Materials required: yellow fabric with black or brown polkadots; black yarn; black embroidery thread; scraps of black felt; scrap of yellow yarn; fiberfill stuffing.

LITTLE PLAID TRAIN:

Materials required: white rickrack; cotton fabric in red plaid; white felt; scrap of blue felt; fiberfill stuffing.

A Patchwork Christmas or a Country Christmas enables us to cash in on antiques, quilting, country jams and jellies, attic treasures, all the old-fashioned products, as well as the newest styling concepts. Most such products will be fashioned from cottons and often from scraps, but such a theme as this makes a budget restriction into an asset. A good item to raffle might be a patchwork quilt.

Old-fashioned, down-on-the-farm ideas for a bazaar either in the spring or at holidaytime enables us to feature fruits and vegetables of all kinds as decorative items. The watermelon and strawberry are of Christmas colors, and the mushroom, eggplant, purple onion, artichoke, and asparagus all have the feel and colors of spring. (See Plate 40.)

MUSHROOM POT HOLDER

Materials required: white, dark brown, and tan felt.

If the new zigzag sewing machine is used on the two inside edges of the inner mushroom shapes (white and light brown edges), this is a stunning product. (See Plate 40.)

STRAWBERRY POT HOLDER

Materials required: small pieces of white and green felt; yellow embroidery thread; cut-up blanket or mattress padding for pad insert; red cotton poplin fabric. (See Plate 40.)

ARTICHOKE POT HOLDER

Materials required: three shades of green felt. (See Plate 40.)

WATERMELON POT HOLDER (PLATE 40)

Materials required: red, green, white felt; a small piece of black felt.

PURPLE ONION POT HOLDER (PLATE 40)

Materials required: dark purple and hot pink felt; small square of white felt; hot pink embroidery thread.

YELLOW ASPARAGUS POT HOLDER (PLATE 40)

Materials required: lemon yellow, kelly green, and orange felt; orange yarn; orange embroidery thread.

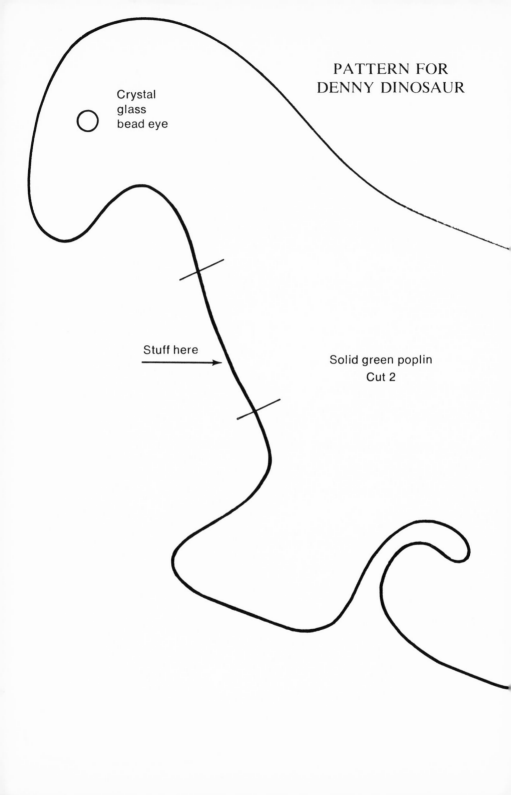

PATTERN FOR
DENNY DINOSAUR

Crystal
glass
bead eye

Stuff here

Solid green poplin
Cut 2

PATTERN FOR
SNOOPY SNAIL

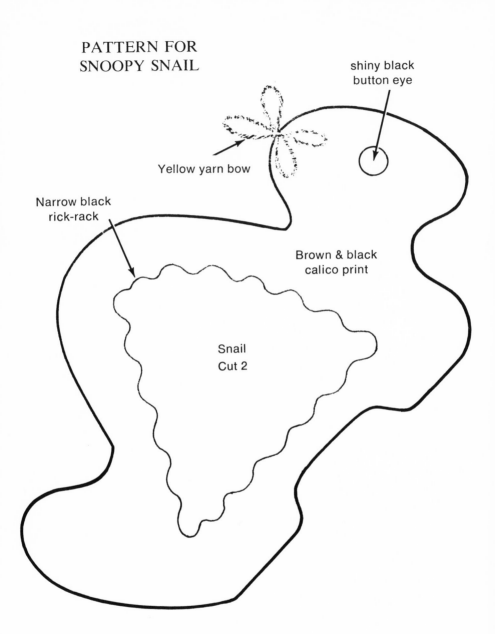

shiny black
button eye

Yellow yarn bow

Narrow black
rick-rack

Brown & black
calico print

Snail
Cut 2

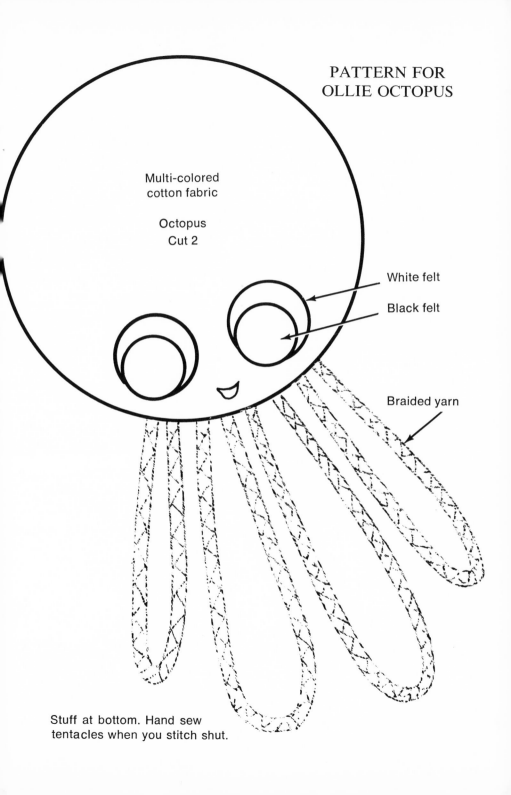

PATTERN FOR
OLLIE OCTOPUS

Multi-colored
cotton fabric

Octopus
Cut 2

White felt

Black felt

Braided yarn

Stuff at bottom. Hand sew
tentacles when you stitch shut.

PATTERN FOR
RONNIE RABBIT

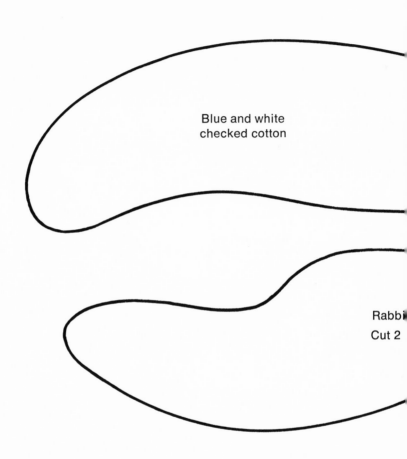

Blue and white
checked cotton

Rabbi

Cut 2

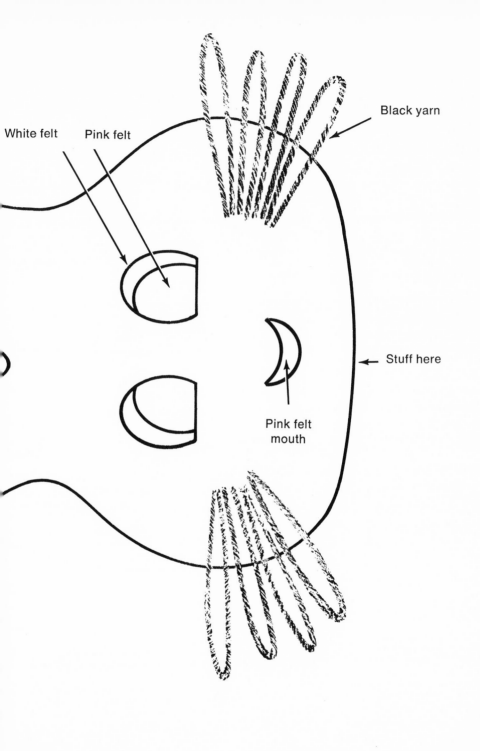

White felt   Pink felt

Black yarn

Stuff here

Pink felt
mouth

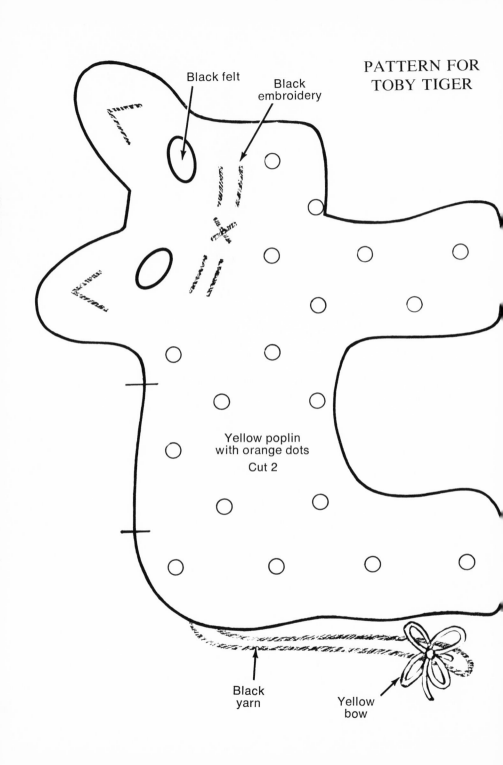

PATTERN FOR
TOBY TIGER

Black felt

Black
embroidery

Yellow poplin
with orange dots
Cut 2

Black
yarn

Yellow
bow

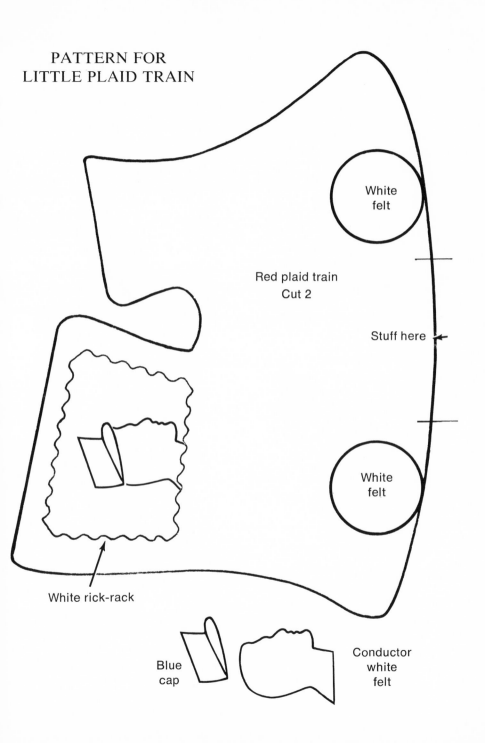

PATTERN FOR
LITTLE PLAID TRAIN

White
felt

Red plaid train
Cut 2

Stuff here

White
felt

White rick-rack

Blue
cap

Conductor
white
felt

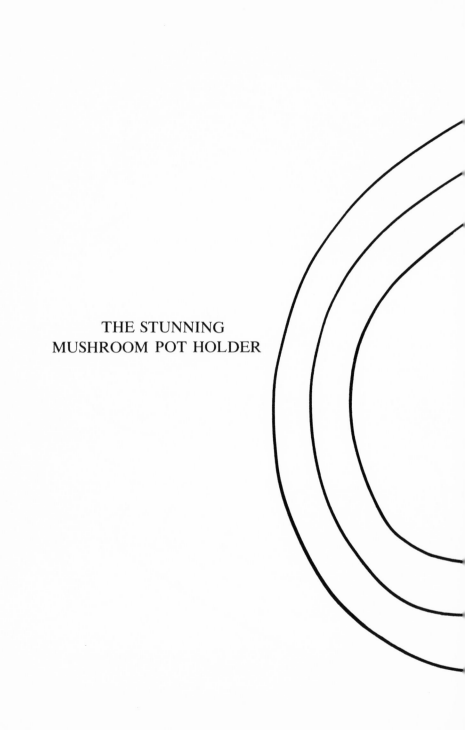

THE STUNNING
MUSHROOM POT HOLDER

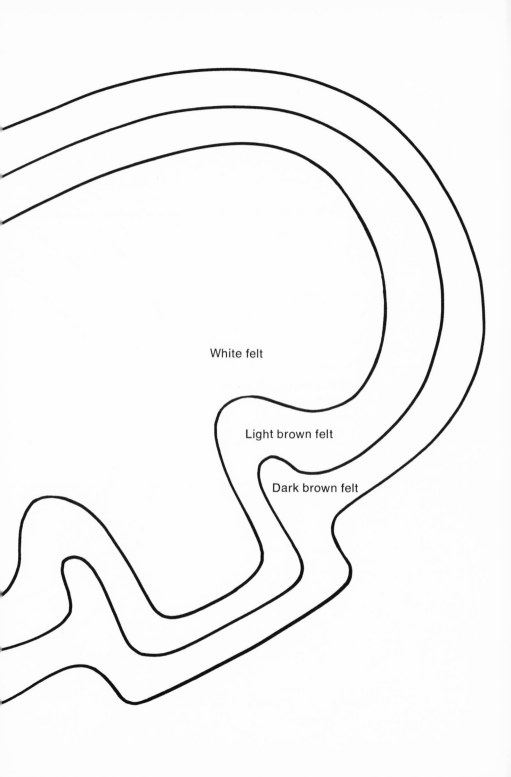

White felt

Light brown felt

Dark brown felt

PATTERN FOR THE STRAWBERRY
POT HOLDER

Green
felt
leaves
Cut 3

White
felt
flower

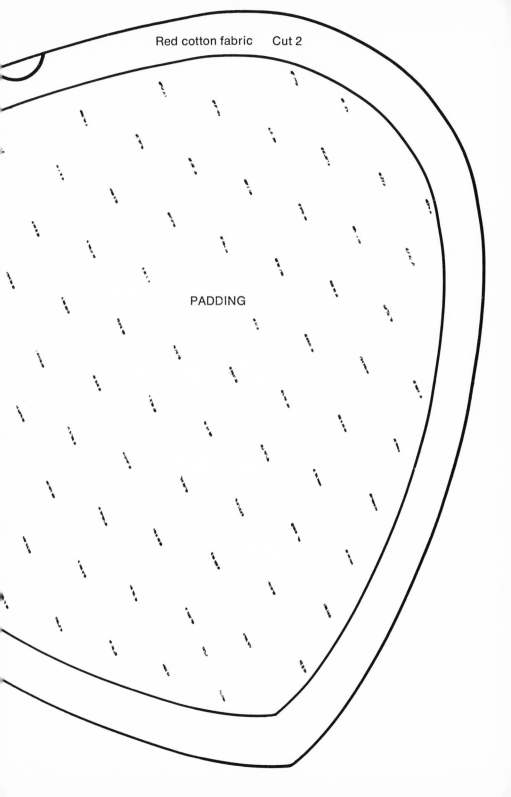

Red cotton fabric   Cut 2

PADDING

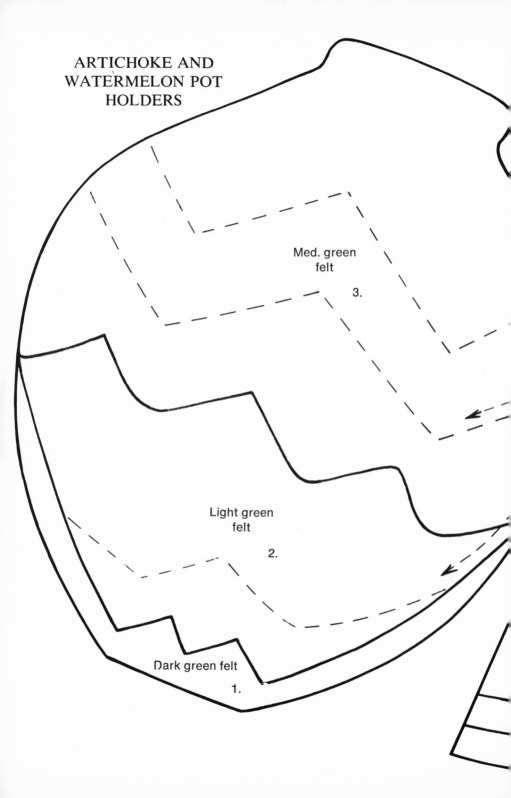

ARTICHOKE AND
WATERMELON POT
HOLDERS

Med. green
felt

3.

Light green
felt

2.

Dark green felt

1.

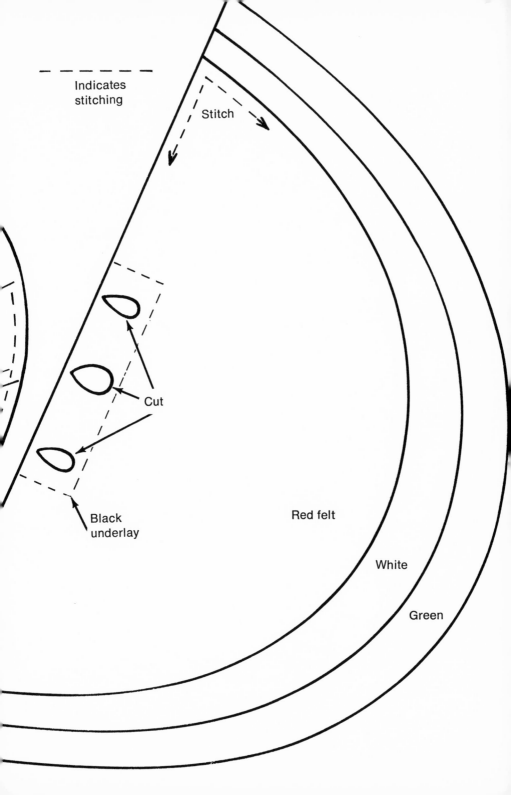

Indicates stitching

Stitch

Cut

Black underlay

Red felt

White

Green

PATTERN FOR
PURPLE ONION POT HOLDER

White
felt

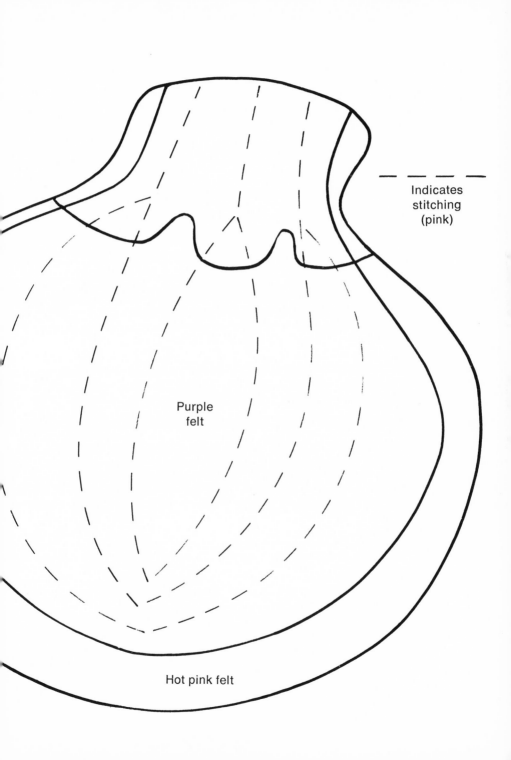

Indicates
stitching
(pink)

Purple
felt

Hot pink felt

THE YELLOW ASPARAGUS POT HOLDER

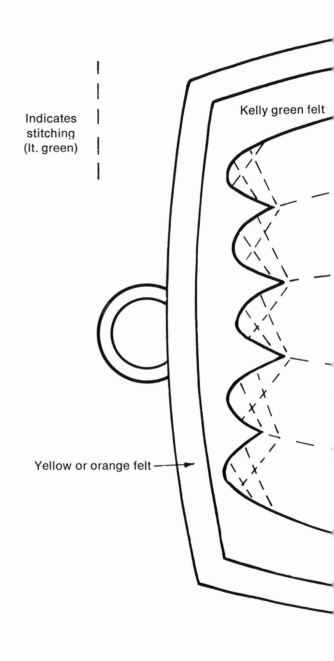

Indicates
stitching
(lt. green)

Kelly green felt

Yellow or orange felt

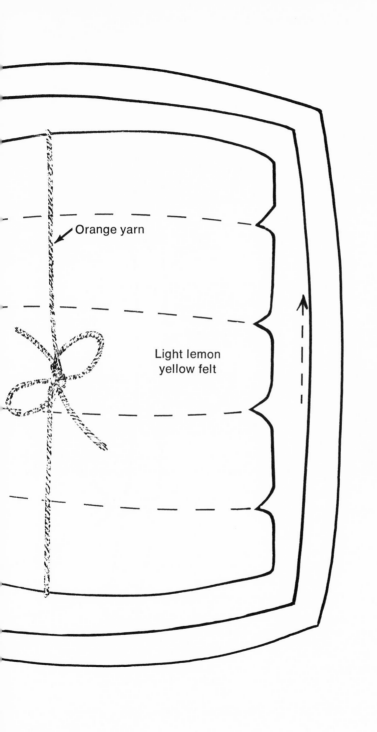

Orange yarn

Light lemon
yellow felt

PLATE 40. Smart kitchen pot holders made from the patterns in this chapter.

Another extremely versatile product for either a Christmas or spring bazaar is the Night-light Lady with the Fringy Hair. She's a plus for any powder room or she serves as an excellent bath or bedroom night-light. For a Christmas product, purchase a regular beige night-light with a small ridge down the center. (For spring, use pink or light blue lights.) These lights are commonly found in any hardware store. The ridge forms the nose; and she looks, when finished, like the lady in Plate 41.

NIGHT-LIGHT LADY

Materials required for a Christmas Night-light Lady: Beige night-light of the type that will plug into a wall socket, preferably one with a vertical ridge down the center; red and green felt; 4″ black fringe; narrow black rickrack for eyes; small cluster of artificial flowers, either felt or straw; narrow ribbon.

Materials required for a Springtime Night-light Lady: light blue night-light; pink and blue felt; 4″ white fringe; cluster of flowers; black rickrack; narrow ribbon.

Glue approximately 4 inches of long gold, white, or black fringe around her face (front side of night-light). Trim the fringe to form facial area. Add red felt mouth (use paper punch). Add black baby rickrack for eyelashes. For her hat, cut large oval from pink felt to pattern, the three-quarters oval of pastel blue felt. (Use red and green felt at Christmas.) Glue blue felt piece to lower part of pink oval, spread out lengthwise, and fold back front pink portion to form hat brim. Glue on flowers for decoration; add narrow blue velvet ribbon about neck area for scarf.

PLATE 41. The versatile Night-light Lady with the Fringy Hair.

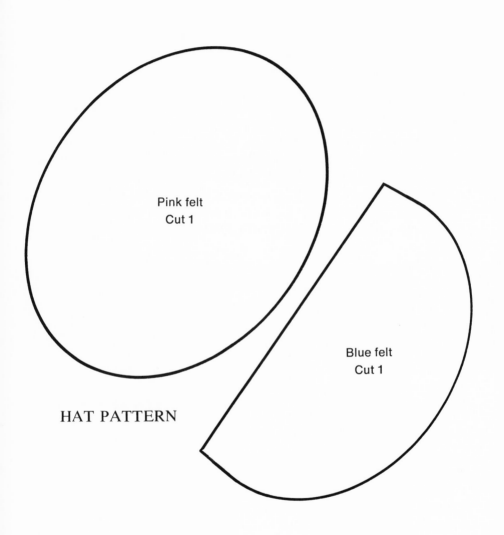

Pink felt
Cut 1

Blue felt
Cut 1

HAT PATTERN

One of the present-day realities we must deal with is the fact that more than 50 percent of American women hold down jobs outside their homes. This will inevitably affect the amount of personnel available to work on a community fund-raising event, but it need not dampen your enthusiasm with regard to your options for a bazaar. The women you want to be involved are not disinterested or unwilling to serve; women will always be interested in good goals and in creative handwork.

The solution lies in your ability to adapt your project to what they can conceivably handle. In other words, *cater to them*, and you will get the job done. This will result in your developing ways to get your projects available to them so that they can work at home in their spare time or in the evenings, and your ideas will need to be portable. Those women who are available during the day are best used in cutting, organizing, and assembling the things that you are going to sew or make. A prepared unit can be placed in a plastic bag ready to be picked up for completion by those who must work at home. Regularly scheduled club meetings or after-church coffees are a handy way to dispense your products to this work force. They can then take them home, returning the finished merchandise on the following Sunday or meeting date.

The secret is planning, organization, and, finally, communication. A completed sampling showing exactly what you wish to have duplicated is easily absorbed and comprehended by your work-at-home assistants. And if you want the job done right, *you* will be there to answer any questions.

One project which lends itself beautifully to the work-at-home creativity of your membership is the originally designed music box. All the ceramic and plastic figures utilized in the scenes set upon plywood bases (with music boxes added) shown in Plates 42–45 were ordered most inexpensively from the Maid of Scandinavia catalog. Music boxes and plywood bases are available at most hobby shops or from the Pink Sleigh (see Chapter X). There is good profit in music boxes at any sale, and they are great fun to make, for *you* are the designer!

Be comforted in the knowledge that some household objects

PLATE 42.   The Old Woman in the Shoe is a perennial children's favorite at any time of the year.

PLATES 43 AND 44.   Spring music boxes.

PLATE 45.   The Christmas Band can be put together very inexpensively.

PLATE 46. A Santa doll anyone could love (see Chapter X, Christmas Products to Make).

PLATE 47. A sewing case whose uniqueness lies in the folding.

are always in demand. A sewing case, a baby gift, a pincushion, a flyswatter, a Santa doll—such geegaws are timeless. They perform a useful function, and their designs can be manipulated to suit your interests. (See Plates 46 and 47.)

SEWING CADDY

Materials required: quilted calico fabric; color-coordinated cotton poplin for the lining; thimble; small scissors; straight pins; safety pins; needle threader; cardboard wound with thread; packet of needles; one giant dress snap.

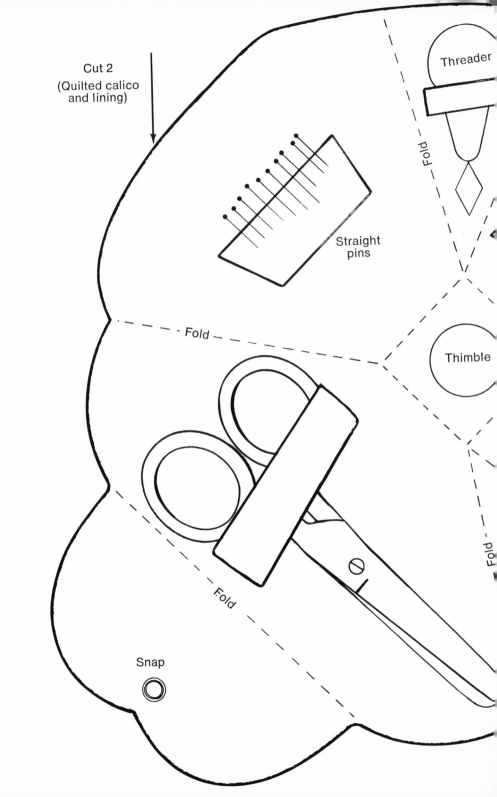

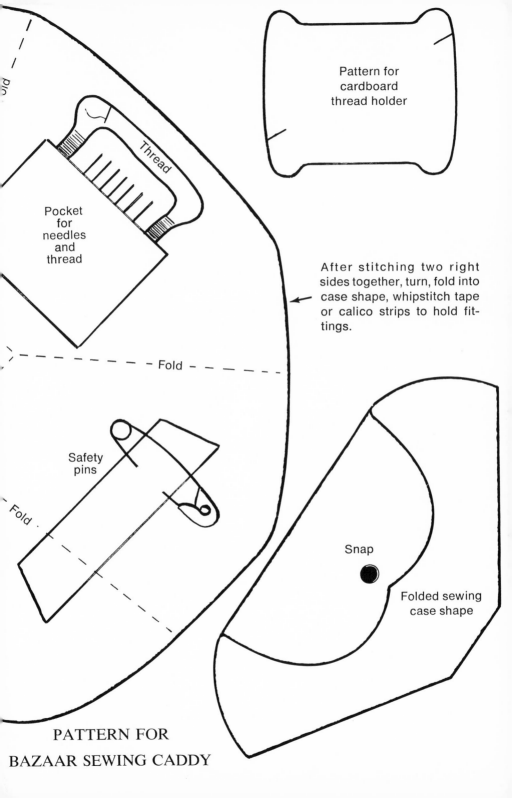

Pattern for
cardboard
thread holder

Thread

Pocket
for
needles
and
thread

fold

After stitching two right
sides together, turn, fold into
case shape, whipstitch tape
or calico strips to hold fit-
tings.

– Fold – – –

Safety
pins

Fold

Snap

Folded sewing
case shape

PATTERN FOR
BAZAAR SEWING CADDY

DIRECTIONS FOR BIRD NEST ORNAMENT
(PLATE 48)

Fashion a circle of package excelsior, and clip it firmly in a round shape with center depression by using clip clothespins. Spray generously with spray starch, and let stand overnight. On following day, spray wooden clothespin and bird nest with gold spray paint. Glue nest to top of clothespin, and fasten stuffed red cardinal to side of nest. Multicolor large wooden beads make eggs for a realistic touch.

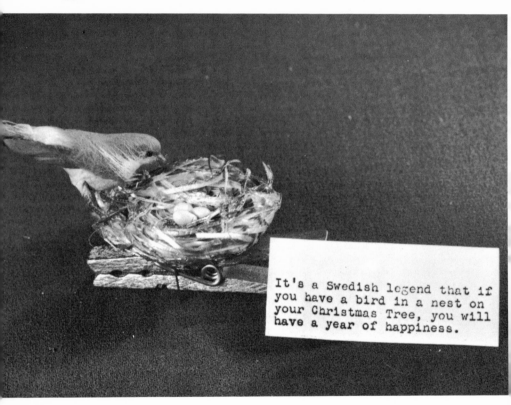

It's a Swedish legend that if you have a bird in a nest on your Christmas Tree, you will have a year of happiness.

PLATE 48. An ecologically perfect tree ornament fashioned from reused package excelsior.

DIRECTIONS FOR THE SHELL "ANGEL IN FLIGHT" ORNAMENT (PLATE 5, CHAPTER I)

A lacy, fan-shaped shell makes the gown for this lovely angel. If one lives by the sea, this is a natural. I purchase my shells by the packet at hobby shops or by the pound at the shore. Make a dozen of these at a time; it will take two or three days to accomplish the glueing process by various stages. First, glue a cloth-covered head with painted face to the center of the top of the shell, securing on back side the wound glued wire from the head, with a clothespin to dry overnight. From the colors of the angel's hat, pick up the colors in the brilliant jewels which decorate her gown. Thus, the angel is accented with purple, red, blue, green, or yellow. Hatted angel faces are sold by packet from the Maid of Scandinavia catalog, 12 to a set. I use white or pastel netting leaves for wings, but gold metallic leaves would make the wings for a lovely angel. Silver leaves are also available.

FELT SNOWMAN ORNAMENT WITH CANDY CANE (PLATE 49)

Materials required: white, red and black felt; one candy cane; gold cord for hanger; blue and black sequins; red sequins in moon and star shapes; tiny crystal beads. Eyes are made of red star sequins, nose of a blue star sequin. The mouth is a red, moon shaped sequin and the buttons are black sequins.

Whipstitch around external surfaces of snowman, leaving space under scarf for candy cane insertion. Place white felt snowman inside 2 black hats, gluing down, but first tack down gold cord onto tip of snowman. When sewing on sequins, add a tiny white crystal bead at the center. It gives a snowy sparkle to the finished ornament. Glue on red scarf.

FELT HOBBY HORSE ORNAMENT WITH CANDY CANE (PLATE 49)

Materials required: white felt, thin gold rickrack; green sequins for eyes; red fringe for mane; gold cord; candy cane.

Black felt
Cut 2

FELT SNOWMAN ORNAMENT WITH CANDY CANE

Eyes—red star sequin
Nose—blue sequin
Buttons—black sequins
Mouth—red moon, sequin

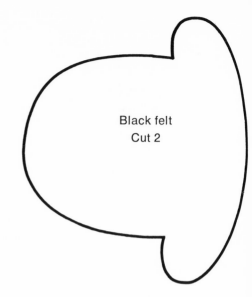

Red felt
Cut 1

Hanger

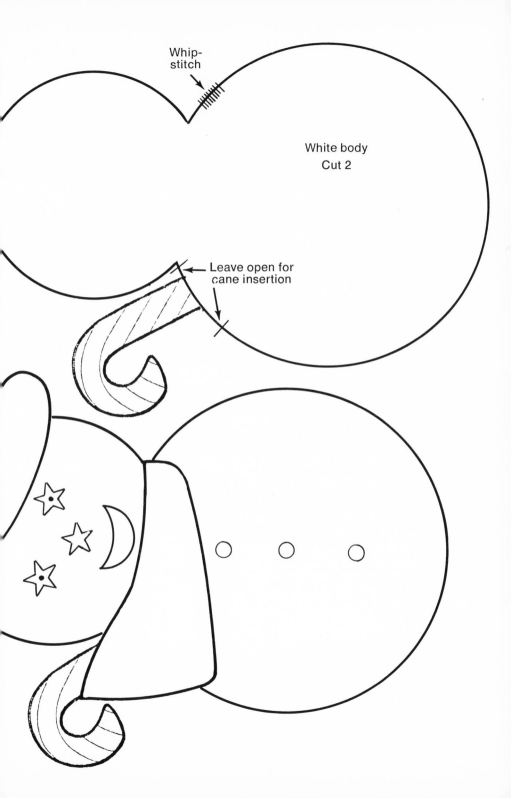

Whip-
stitch

White body
Cut 2

Leave open for
cane insertion

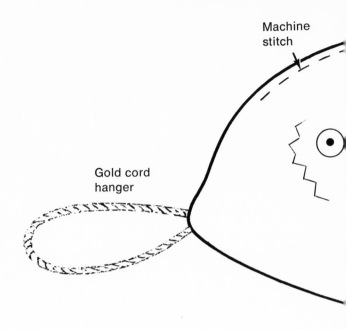

Machine
stitch

Gold cord
hanger

FELT HOBBY HORSE ORNAMENT WITH CANDY CANE

Materials needed:
White felt
Thin gold rick-rack
Green sequins
Red fringe
Gold cord
Candy cane

Eye is green sequin
Mane is red fringe

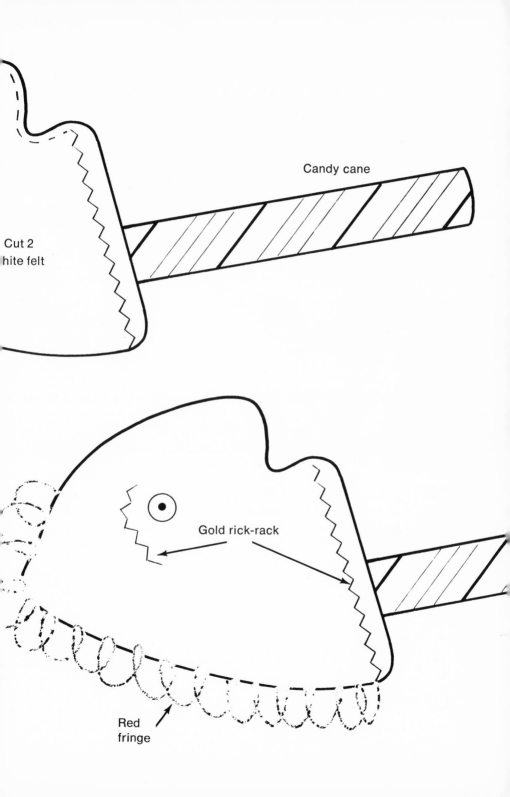

Candy cane

Cut 2
hite felt

Gold rick-rack

Red
fringe

PLATE 49. Ornaments including candy-cane insertion.

WHITE CLEANING-BAG WREATH (PLATE 50)

Materials required: one large wreath requires approximately 32 large (coat) cellophane clothing bags which are devoid of printing or advertisement unless writing is white. These may be ordered by the roll through professional cleaners. You will need large quantities of white pipe cleaners of average length (7 inches), which should be cut in half. Use a wire coat hanger to form wreath.

Secure a strip of plastic around the hook to cover it, grounding at base of loop where it joins circle of wreath with a tightly wound pipe cleaner.

Next, lay 8 bags one on top of the other. Fold in half, and in half again, lengthwise. Cut into 1½″ strips (8 pieces in each strip), separate the strips, and put over the hands as you would to wind yarn; then twist and fold in half, repeating two more times. Now twist on a pipe cleaner, and cut plastic loops. You will want a stem of pipe cleaner about 2¼″ long left at one end. Twist these pipe cleaners around coat hanger placing cut loops close together. Decorate with small velvet bows (secured by fastening onto pipe cleaners which in turn are wound onto wreath), artificial holly, Christmas velvet balls, or whatever suits your fancy. These wreaths are milky white in color and are stunning.

PLATE 50. The glamorous snowy-white Cleaning
Bag Wreath.

"WINSOME MISS" FIRESIDE BROOM
(PLATE 51)

Materials required: one small *red*-handled child's broom (available in variety stores for about 79 cents); large piece of red felt; one 4" styrofoam ball; a sprig of artificial holly; scraps of black and red felt.

Cut a piece of felt 18" long and 4½" wide. Fringe ends. This will form the shawl. Drape around broom brush as in Plate 51, fastening in back. Attach piece of plastic holly with safety pin in front center. After forcing a pencil through styro ball for headpiece (to make application to broom handle easier), slide head ball onto broom. Decorate face with 2 round black felt eyes, triangular red nose, and red felt mouth (with smile). Cut cardboard piece for hat shape according to pattern; duplicate in red felt (noting fold line), allowing ¼" larger border line for felt than for cardboard, for the felt will have to cover the cardboard; then whipstitch around edges of hat. Cut center hole to go over stick. In addition, cut 2" length of red felt to go around broom handle at top of hat, and sew on small piece of additional holly. The basic broom costs at retail about 90 cents in the New York area.

DIRECTIONS FOR THE LOVELY PAPER-TUBE TREE
(PLATE 52)

(Mantelpiece or table decoration)

Materials required: This lovely decoration requires 35 five-inch pieces of mailing tubing or 1-inch-wide cut tubing used by hospitals and institutions which purchase rubber sheeting; 56 tiny ball ornaments, red, green, and blue (boxed at dime store); gold spray paint; glue; small pieces of blue, red or green felt for base.

Cut cast-off roller tubing to pieces of equal length (approximately 5 inches). Form base by gluing 3 tubes together to make bottom row; form next two rows by gluing 2 more tubes in first row. Put this aside. Separately form body of tree by gluing to-

PLATE 51. The Winsome Miss Christmas Fireside Broom.

PLATE 52. A Christmas bazaar product that shines like a prism is the extremely effective Paper-Tube Tree.

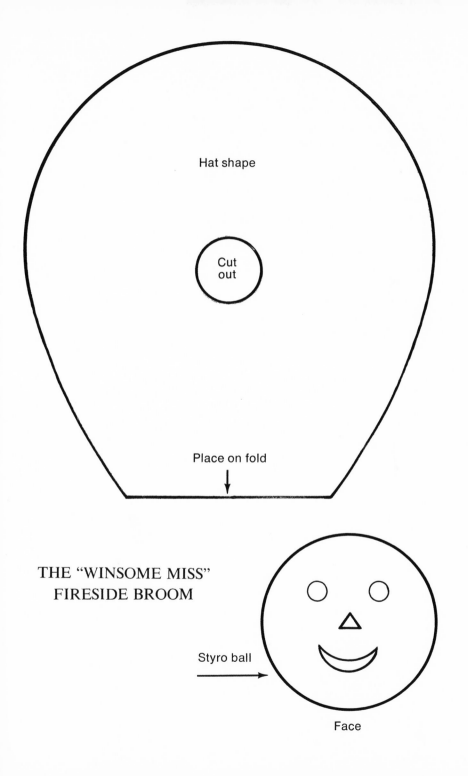

Hat shape

Cut out

Place on fold

THE "WINSOME MISS"
FIRESIDE BROOM

Styro ball

Face

gether 7 tubes in a row; then 6 in next row, 5 in following row, pyramiding until top is a single tube. Spray gold, glue and all. When completely dry, glue alternating colored small ornaments into entire circumference of holes at either end of tubes, forming multicolored tree. Last of all, glue small rectangular felt base on bottom 3 tubes for flatter surface.

DIRECTIONS FOR THE PINE CONE MAIDENS
A CHRISTMAS TABLE DECORATION

(As seen in Chapter I, Plate 4)

Collect firm pine cones, 2½ to 3 inches in height. Taking two of similar proportion, lock them together so that they stand easily entwined. Glue, wherever they touch and interlock, with transparent glue which dries clear. Taking 2 wired cloth-covered faces, fasten them by winding around top tips of pine cones; then glue down securely. Take a green and red 6-inch strip of pinked felt about 1 inch wide, and tie a muffler about the necks of the little maidens, one green, one red. This will hide all wiring. One could add a red and green sprayed acorn top as hat to their heads, adding red and green brilliants for hat decoration. With bright red nail polish, add two layers of polish to the bottommost pine layer, which then resemble little shoes. Cloth-covered faces are in Maid of Scandinavia catalog, ordered by dozen.

DIRECTIONS FOR THE SWEET-GUM
WREATH ORNAMENT (PLATE 53)

Materials required: seven sweet-gum seedpods; gold or silver metallic spray paint; silver or gold color cord; imitation "jewels" in brilliant colors; velvet ribbon in matching color.

Form a circle of about 7 of the seedpods of similar size, glue them to each other securely. Then spray them liberally on both sides with metallic gold paint. When all is completely dry, adhere several brilliant red jewels strategically about its circumference;

PLATE 53. The Cypress Pine Cone Tree flanked by sweet-gum seed-pod wreath ornaments.

then attach a thin, gold hanger. It is equally attractive with other colored jewels, or if sprayed silver, use shocking pink or aqua jewels, and a silver cord. Add a narrow velvet matching colored bow to complete the wreath.

DIRECTIONS FOR THE CYPRESS PINE CONE TREE AND/OR MUSIC BOX (PLATE 53)

Materials required: 15 pine cones; white spray paint; gold metallic spray paint; glue; plywood cut in circle shape (5″ diameter); white felt; gilt; brass snowflakes; gold braid; gold foil; metallic gold bow; music box (optional).

These lightweight cones are sold by the dozen at the Pink Sleigh, which imports them from Italy, and they are inexpensive. Forming a circle of 7 of these flowerlets, glued together, make the base for a pyramid of these, the second layer resting on the joined area of the first layer underneath. The second layer requires four, the third layer three, and a single upright cone forms the top. Spray the glued pyramid with white paint, and when all glue and paint have hardened, lightly dust with a quick pass-over of gold metallic spray paint. Mount the tree on a 5-inch wide circle of plywood, which has been covered, top and bottom, with a layer of white felt, pre-dusted with gilt (available at many dime stores). A packet of brass gold snowflakes completes the decorations, strategically glued about the tree. Attractive gold finishing braid goes about the base of plywood, and a Swiss music box which plays "White Christmas" may be mounted behind the tree to add interest to this gift item. Cover tiny pieces of cardboard with gold foil, and place under the tree, decorated with miniature metallic gold bows from the Pink Sleigh. This is also very effective when done in light blue with pearl snowflakes. Any holes between cones may be filled with tiny gold regular gilt cones which come wired in bunches.

DIRECTIONS FOR VELVET STRAWBERRY ORNAMENT AND/OR PINCUSHION

(As seen in Plate 2, Chapter I)

Materials required: one 2-inch styrofoam egg; 1 piece red velveteen 3½ by 3½ inches; 8 green velvet wired leaves; 12 seed pearls and 12 short straight pins; 1 brass circlet and gold hanging cord; glue (Sobo or Elmer's).

Directions: Cut piece of red or shocking pink velvet or velveteen 3½ by 3½ inches. On the wrong side, block out two lines into four equal squares.

Put dots of glue on four outside points, and one in the center.

164

Place styro egg point in exact center of velveteen square. Bring up flaps of velveteen from four *centers* (*rather than* corners), and secure with sequin pins into egg. Glue insides of four corners,

and bring to center top (later covered with green leaves).

Secure and flatten folds of velveteen with sequin pins inserted into pearls. Cascade leaves in two layers, tops overlapping under-leaves, and glue down. Pull cord hanger, knot end down, through brass circlet, and secure to strawberry top with pearl-topped pin (hatpin). A white plastic or ceramic bowl with holly interspersed with strawberries makes an excellent display for the sale of these ornaments or pincushions.

PURPLE COW REFRIGERATOR DECORATION

> *"I never saw a purple cow,*
> *I never hope to see one;*
> *But I can tell you, anyhow,*
> *I'd rather see than be one!"*

Materials required: dark purple felt; light purple felt; strong gold cord; rolling eyes; alphabet macaroni; large, round black sequins; bell; small gold sequins; one magnetic flexible strip with adhesive backing. This felt cow is attractive done in black and white, as well as in purples. It adheres to the enameled surface

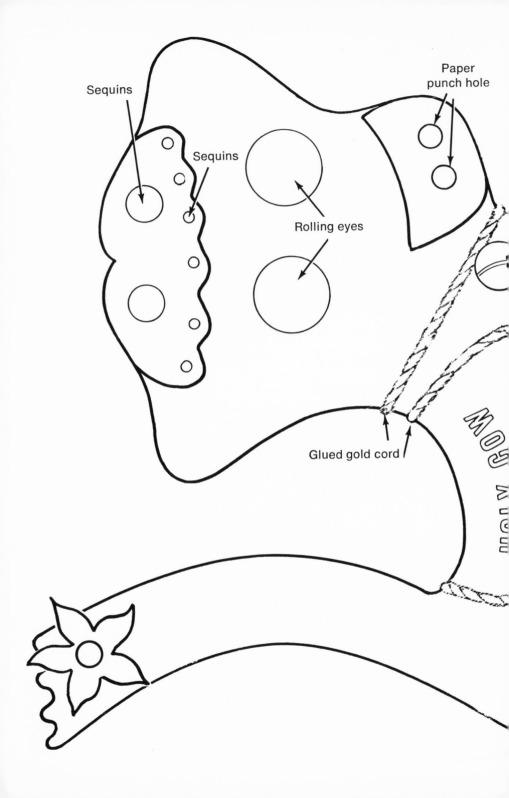

PURPLE COW REFRIGERATOR DECORATION

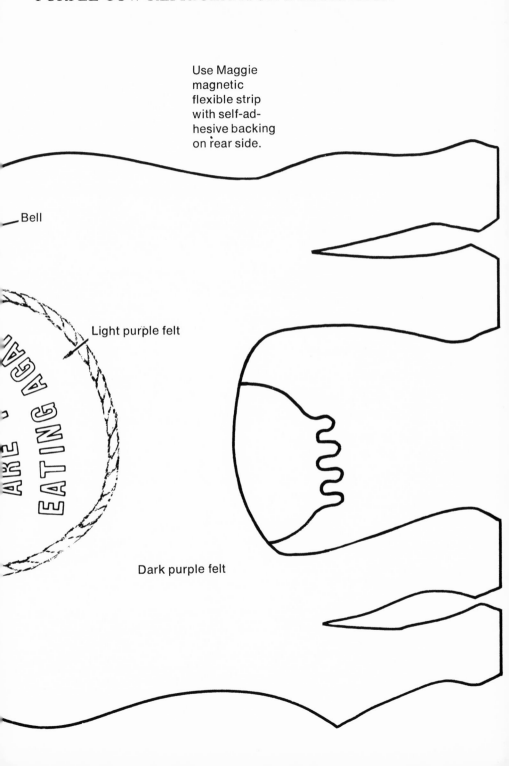

Use Maggie
magnetic
flexible strip
with self-ad-
hesive backing
on rear side.

Bell

Light purple felt

ARE
EATING AGA

Dark purple felt

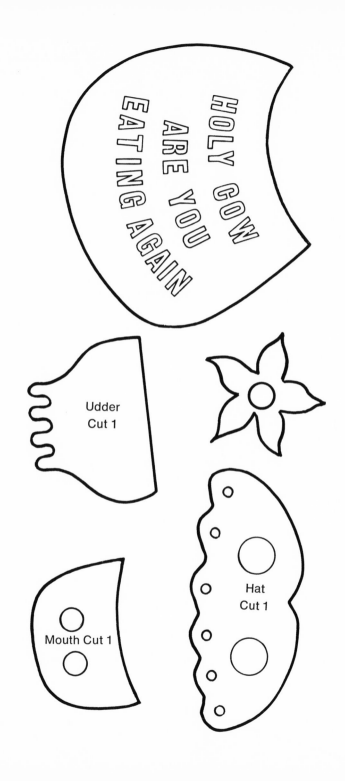

of the refrigerator door through the use of magnetized strips placed on the back of the felt cut-out cow. It is adorned with sequins large and small and large rolling eyes, which are glued on. The cow's nostrils are cut with a paper punch. The lettering is done with glued on, painted alphabet macaroni from chain stores. It is a very brisk seller mounted against a piece of cardboard and covered with Saran wrap.

PASTEL BUNNY PURSE

Materials required: felt in a pastel color; white, pink, and black scraps of felt; a printed or embroidered pastel braid for handle; strands of black carpet thread.

This is a great favorite with the kindergarten crowd. Quickly cut out, it should be sewn around three-quarters of its outer egg-shaped edge. Black carpet thread makes the whiskers. Make it in pale green, yellow, lavender, and pink felt, a deeper pink than the inner ear. The face is always white, inner ear always pink for maximum effect. Handle is best made of braid because felt pulls out of shape.

YELLOW DUCK PENCIL HOLDER

Materials required: one small ruler; four yellow pencils; yellow felt; scraps of white, black, lime green, and orange felt. Fill with four pencils and a ruler. Stitch with orange thread. Catch mouth and feet in seam when stitching.

MORE SPRING-EASTER PRODUCTS TO MAKE: SUNBONNET SUE NEEDLE AND PIN HOLDER

Materials required: yellow felt; light blue narrow satin ribbon; strip of ½" cotton lace; pastel embroidery cotton; white felt; needles/pins in assorted sizes.

Sunbonnet Sue is cut out of pastel yellow felt; sides and bottom are left open. The hat area is whipstitched closed. Her petticoats of white felt are whipstitched in yellow, and gathered lace is across her pantaloon bottoms and gathered also in a circle to

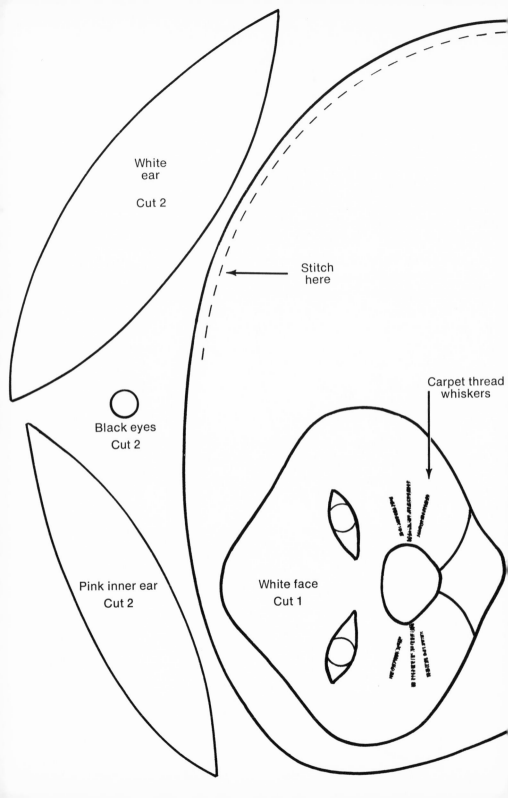

White
ear

Cut 2

Stitch
here

Black eyes
Cut 2

Carpet thread
whiskers

Pink inner ear
Cut 2

White face
Cut 1

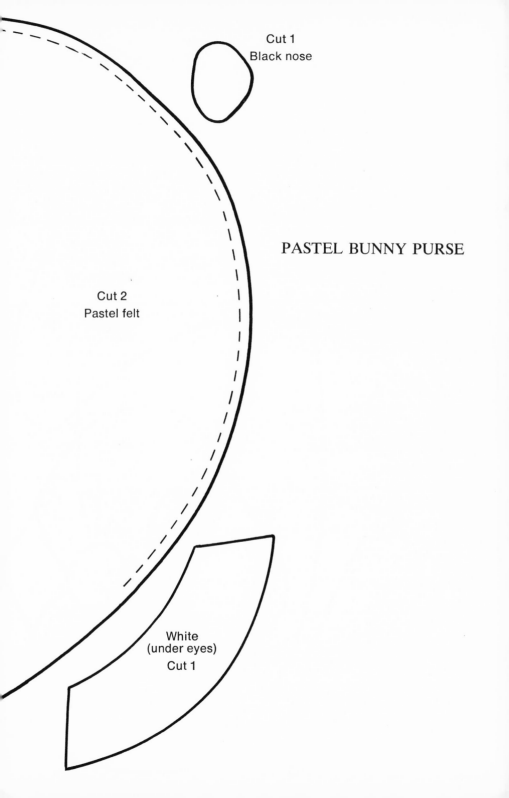

Cut 1
Black nose

PASTEL BUNNY PURSE

Cut 2
Pastel felt

White
(under eyes)
Cut 1

YELLOW FELT
PENCIL HOLDER

Fill with 4 pencils and ruler. Stitch with orange thread. Catch mouth and feet in seam when stitching.

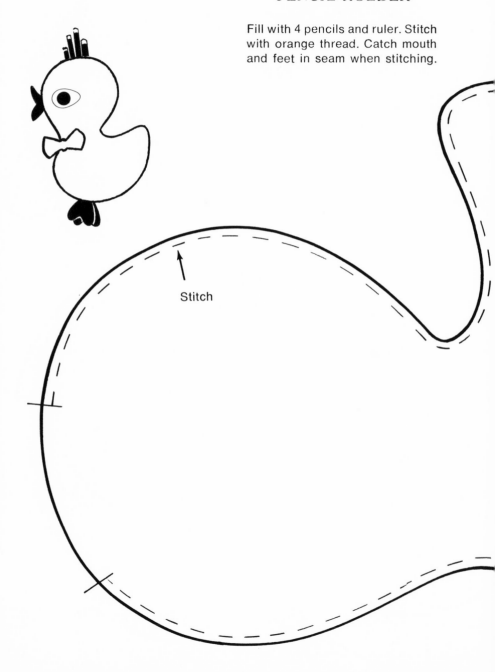

Stitch

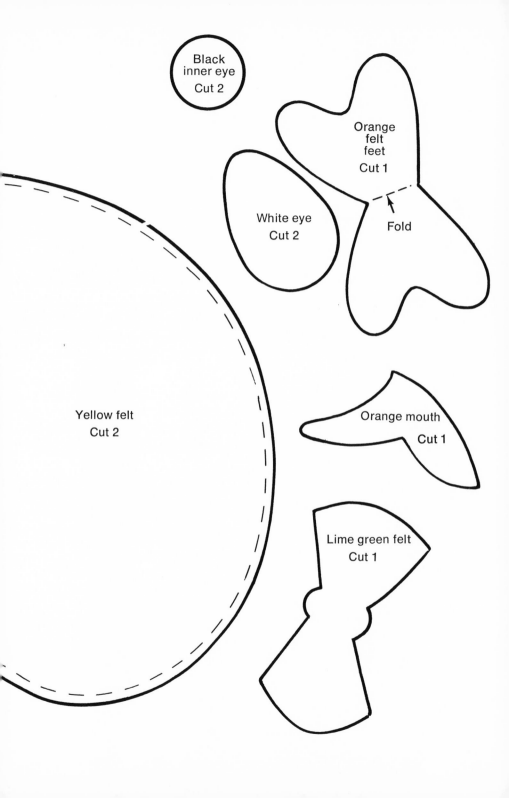

form her corsage. A bow of narrow blue satin ribbon appears to be the ties of her bonnet. French knots are fetching at the center of her lacy corsage. Her underskirts hold several different-sized needles and pins.

BUTTERFLY LIGHT-SWITCH COVER

Materials required: yellow, aqua, and green felt; contrasting sequins; Sobo glue. A product which is a big seller for a teen-ager's room is a gay butterfly cover for a single light switch. The double large butterfly shapes are of the same color; cut out the switch and screw holes, the latter firm and round, using a paper punch inserted from the switch opening. Add wing decoration of contrasting colors. I used shades of yellow, aqua, and green. Sequins were glued onto punched dot wing decorations. Entire product of high-quality felt.

PLATE 53A. Typical Easter bazaar products are offered through the use of posters, here a pastel bunny purse and yellow duck pencil holders.

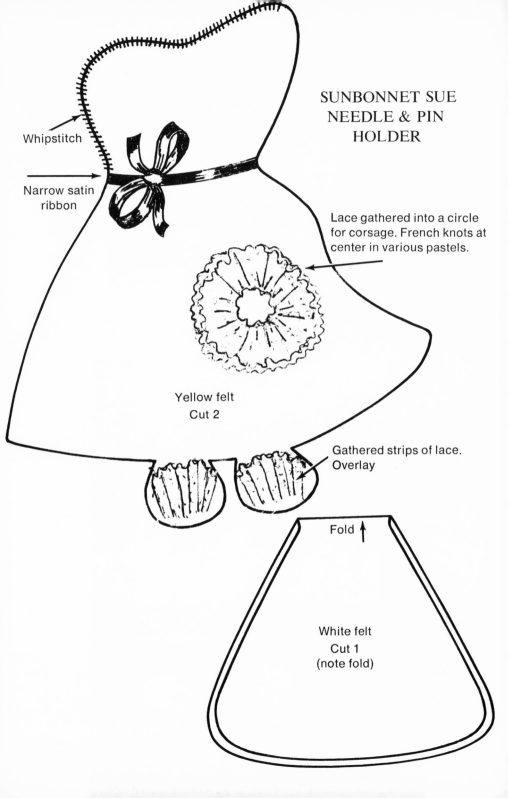

Whipstitch

Narrow satin
ribbon

SUNBONNET SUE
NEEDLE & PIN
HOLDER

Lace gathered into a circle
for corsage. French knots at
center in various pastels.

Yellow felt
Cut 2

Gathered strips of lace.
Overlay

Fold ↑

White felt
Cut 1
(note fold)

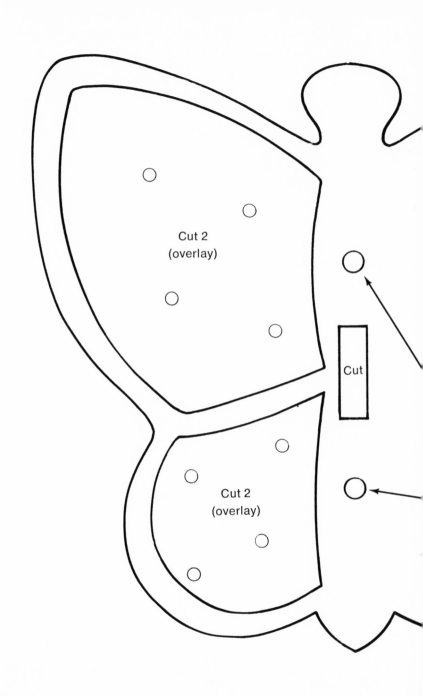

Cut 2
(overlay)

Cut 2
(overlay)

Cut

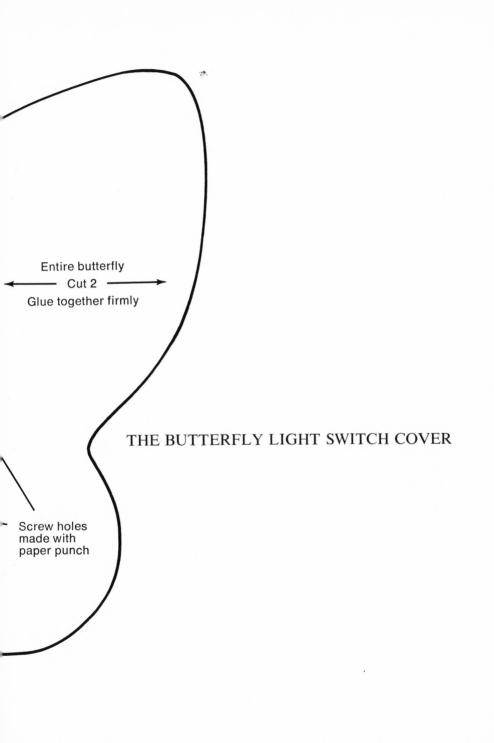

Entire butterfly

◄— Cut 2 —►

Glue together firmly

THE BUTTERFLY LIGHT SWITCH COVER

Screw holes
made with
paper punch

DIRECTIONS FOR A SMALL
KNITTED EASTER BASKET

For a basket 4½ inches long, 2½ inches wide, and 2½ inches tall to tip of handle, use knitting worsted and size 5 or 6 needles, according to tension used in knitting. Time: 1½ hours or less.

Cast on 10 sts. Knitting every row, increase 1 st. in the first and last st. of every other row until you have 20 sts. on needle. Knit 10 rows without increasing; then decrease by knitting 2 sts. together at the beginning and end of every other row until 10 sts. remain on the needle. Bind off, but do not break yarn. Using an 0 crochet hook and a long pipe cleaner (same color as yarn), single crochet the pipe cleaner to under edge of oval piece of knitting (overlapping pipe cleaner at joint.) Fasten off yarn. Bend and roll sides of basket up and flatten ends so it will rest on table without tipping.

Handle: Cast on 3 sts. and knit 40 rows (20 ridges). Bind off, but do not break yarn. Use another pipe cleaner around under edge, single crochet, and finish as for basket. Attach handle to sides of basket. Use a tiny butterfly on handle.

PLATE 54.   Fill basket with May flowers or tiny plastic ducks or bunnies.

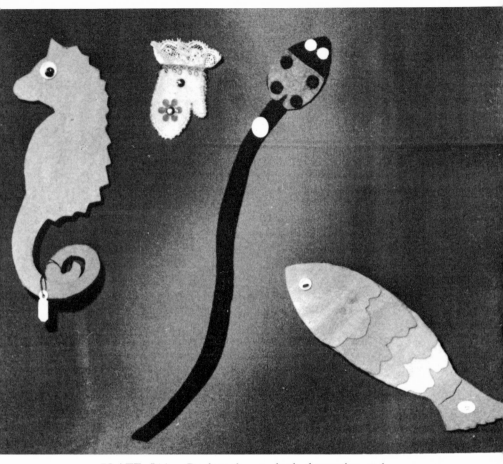

PLATE 54A. Bookmarks are both decorative and useful and can be displayed most attractively to spark sales.

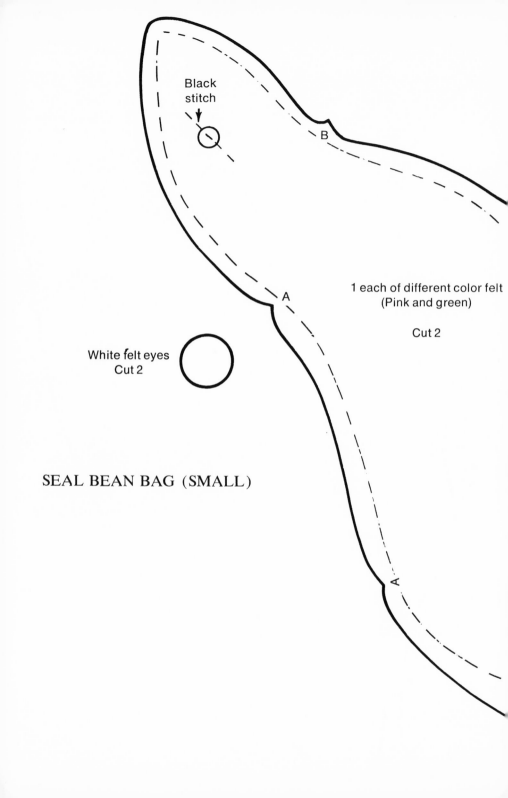

Black stitch

B

1 each of different color felt
(Pink and green)

Cut 2

A

White felt eyes
Cut 2

SEAL BEAN BAG (SMALL)

A

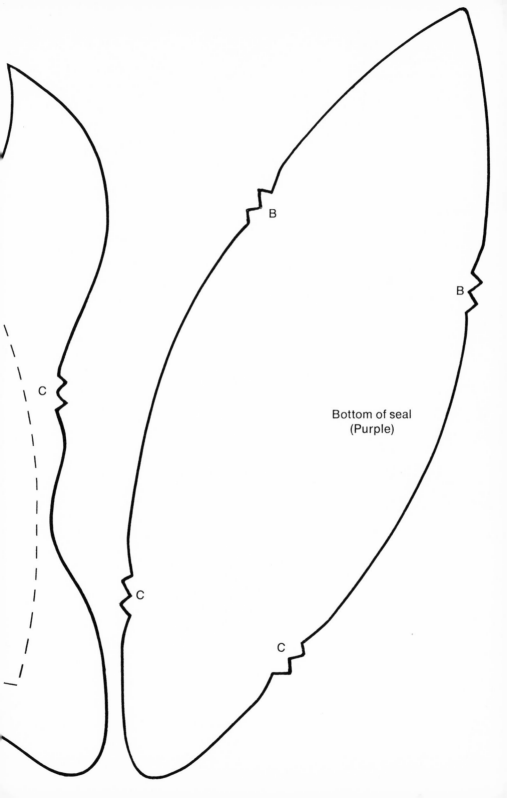

B

B

C

Bottom of seal
(Purple)

C

C

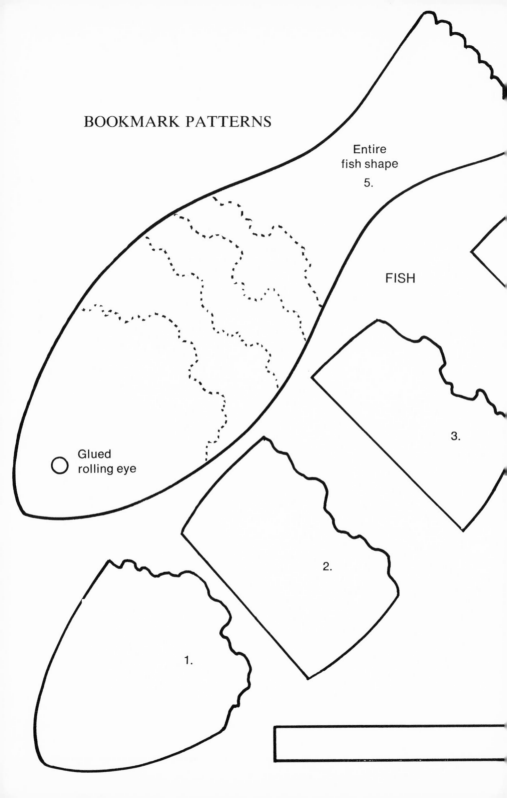

BOOKMARK PATTERNS

Entire
fish shape
5.

FISH

Glued
rolling eye

3.

2.

1.

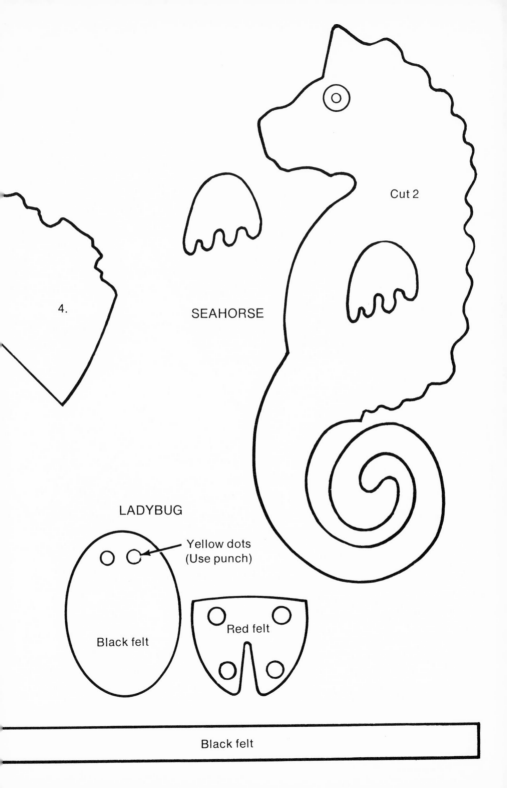

4.

SEAHORSE

Cut 2

LADYBUG

Yellow dots
(Use punch)

Black felt

Red felt

Black felt

It is attractive also as a May basket filled with artificial color-coordinated flowers. *For Christmas bazaars it is lovely done in white yarn and filled with holly and berries.* (See Plate 54.)

SEAL BEANBAG

Materials required: purple, pink, and light green felt; scraps of white felt; beans; white ball fringe; black embroidery thread.

Sew two animal sides together at top, matching notches A to A. On each head side, sew an eye of white felt, using double thread backstitch. Matching notches of B of bottom to B of sides and C of bottom to C of sides, sew bottom to sides, leaving 2-inch opening at tail. Fill head with cotton, rest of body with beans. Sew up bottom. Sew white ball fringe pompon on nose.

BOOKMARKS

FISH:

Materials required: 5 shades of yellow, blue, and green felt; glue; rolling eye.

Cut felt, using a different color for each piece. Glue together so that pieces overlap. Glue on rolling eye.

SEA HORSE:

Materials required: light green and dark blue felt; two contrasting shades of felt for the fins; rolling eye.

Glue together the blue and green felt to form body. Glue fins to body, using contrasting colors for each fin. Glue on eye.

LADYBUG:

Materials required: black, red and yellow felt; strip of black felt.

Glue ladybug shape, made from black felt to one end of the strip of black felt. Glue red pattern piece over the bottom portion of the ladybug body. Glue on dots, made with a hole puncher from the yellow and black felt. Place yellow dots on black portion, black dots on red.

VIII

DEVELOPING NEW LEADS, SPOTTING NEW TRENDS

There is an adage which makes the point that "There is nothing new under the sun!" This is true. The deceiving ingredient in the creation of "something new" lies in the utilization of a new point of view, or a stronger emphasis, or an updated concept. By this I mean the employment of new materials or fabrics, which are often more glamorous, more wrinkleproof, or possibly shinier in texture and different in feel. A few years ago I had very great success with rich, sophisticated velvet and metallic fabrics. Opulence and glamor were a part of the life we sought and the products we bought. Now the trend is toward gingham, calico, simplicity, laciness, and the demure. Patchwork products are the thing; large floppy hats and homecrafted jewelry, knitted and crocheted products are the latest in style. These trends can be exploited to the fullest by those who would run a successful bazaar.

We constantly seek that which is different. Here is where your offerings can shine, for even though you must mass-produce on a small scale, you can personalize a product and make it distinctive, something the large manufacturer cannot do. Often a slogan, alliteration, or a play on words is all that is required to distinguish your idea.

For example, an owl beanbag, bought heavily for gift giving to children and teen-agers as well, was immediately popular because of a single added touch: the glued-in insertion of a popsicle stick complete with a neatly printed oak-tag sign which carried the legend "I love you just the way you are." The owl

PLATE 55. In these times of slogans, try a few!

itself was attractive, but the merchandising with the sign made it an immediate best seller.

The same principle was used at an Easter bazaar where a stuffed, wooden, or plexiglass bunny carried a sign which read: "You're Nobunny Till Somebunny Loves You" (see Plate 55). Thus, a product is new because it carries a slogan.

WISE OWL BEANBAG

Materials required: brown poplin (or strong cotton material); beans; white and black felt; orange cotton poplin; brown felt for the wings.

After experiencing the successes to be achieved at Christmas bazaars by utilizing the principle of the old German ornament created by cutting a window in a piece of imitation velvet fruit, and inserting a winter scene, we adapted the same idea for Easter table products, using instead the shiny, plastic fruits for summer

PLATE 56. Spring scenes in miniature.

PLATE 57. A velvet-over-plastic apple, a Christmas scene inside.

PLATE 58. We spelled out to our customers exactly how to use our products by providing a sample Easter table set with coordinated place mats and china.

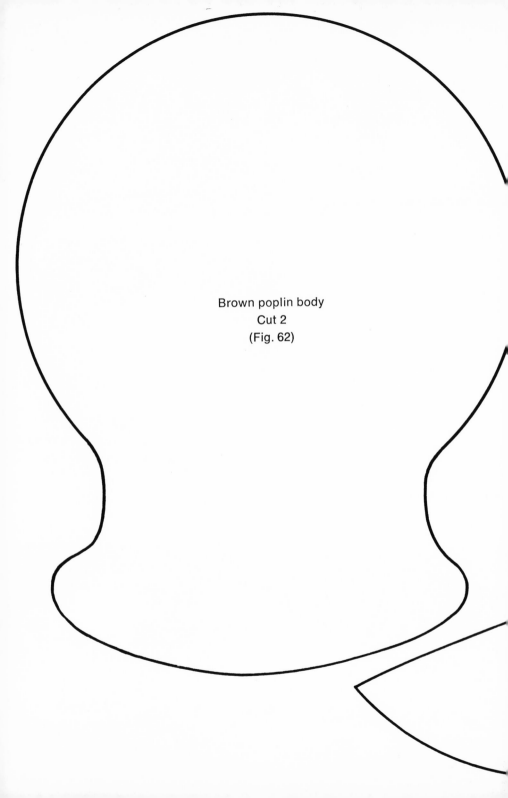

Brown poplin body
Cut 2
(Fig. 62)

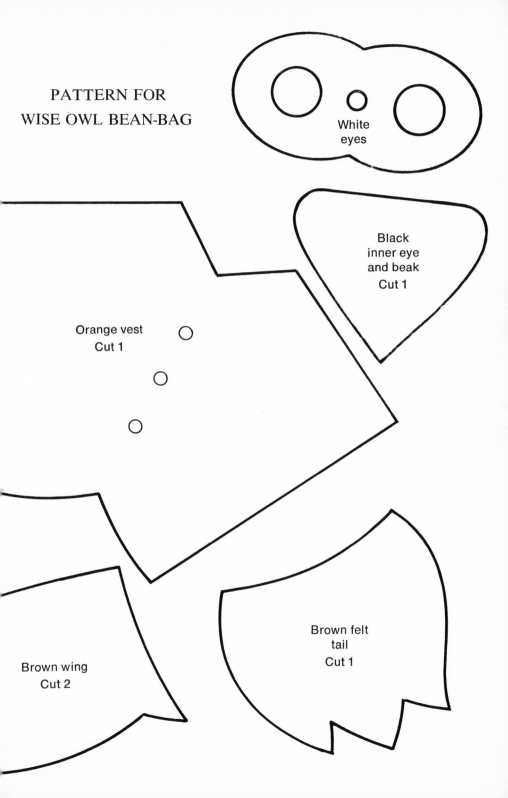

PATTERN FOR
WISE OWL BEAN-BAG

White
eyes

Black
inner eye
and beak
Cut 1

Orange vest
Cut 1

Brown felt
tail
Cut 1

Brown wing
Cut 2

and putting spring and summer scenes inside. Hundreds of these with ladybugs, mushrooms, bunnies, ducks, turtles, and robins as the focal points in the scenes were sold as table decorations and gifts. These miniatures are more and more available through catalogs. (See Plates 56–57.)

In this way, we gave to spring and Easter the same excitement that we gave to Christmas, and it worked!

Another way to make products distinctive is to add the unexpected ingredient, provide an additional service, or call attention to the detail which your competing retail stores cannot afford to offer. For example, a white angora-tipped red knitted stocking ornament which had always been a best seller at Christmas bazaars because it served as the perfect solution to the gift of money took on a smashing new look when we inserted into the top a tiny green felt teddy bear with two tiny red ears. This is a distinctive, cute product (the panda puppet would work equally well). The added cost was infinitesimal, the tiny bear being cut from scraps of felt saved from other projects. This idea will be used again in the spring, when a small felt rabbit and miniature Taiwan basket, shown in Plate 59 and available from Pink Sleigh, will poke out from Easter baskets for children. A miniature stuffed duck, puppy, or kitten made of checked gingham stuffed with a small wad of cotton or Kleenex, ends whipstitched, and placed in a playsuit or bib pocket, provides a built-in toy for the tiny recipient of your merchandise, and the whole concept is extremely pleasing to the eye. (See Plate 31, page 108.)

TINY TEDDY BEAR

Materials required: ears are red felt; bow tie is red yarn. Body is green felt.

DIRECTIONS FOR TINY KNITTED STOCKING ORNAMENT

Use No. 3 needles, bright green or bright red sport yarn; white angora yarn for top, if available.

With white angora yarn, cast on 20 sts. Work in garter stitch for 6 rows (to work garter stitch, knit every row). Break off the

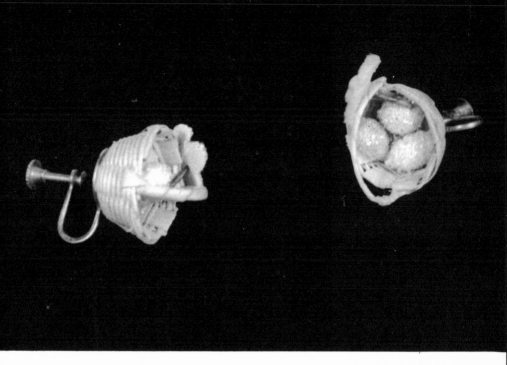

PLATE 59.   Tiny Easter baskets make fetching earrings when filled with flower stamens of pastel colors for eggs.

PATTERN FOR TINY TEDDY BEAR

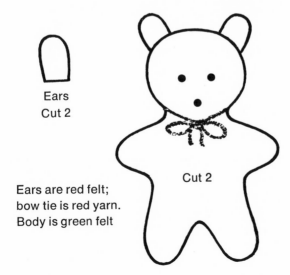

Ears
Cut 2

Ears are red felt;
bow tie is red yarn.
Body is green felt

Cut 2

white yarn, and attach red yarn in first stitch. Use stockinette stitch (knit 1 row, purl 1 row) for the rest. Work 16 rows. On the 17th row, knit 13 sts., turn your work so that the wrong side is facing you, and purl 6 sts. Turn again so the right side is facing you, and knit 6 sts. Turn once more, and purl 6 sts. This is the center of the foot. Turn work. Break off yarn, and tie on just below the last stitch on the right-hand needle. In the space between the two needles, pick up 7 sts. evenly spaced, and place them on the right-hand needle. Knit across the 6 center sts. and pick up 7 sts. on the right-hand needle, and knit to the end of the row. Purl back across all the stitches. Knit 2 sts. together at the beginning and end of the next row (heel shaping) and knit the 2 center sts. together to round off the toe. Continue to decrease in this manner on the knit row only, and work for 6 rows. Bind off, leaving enough yarn to sew up the sole and back seam. Decorate. Tiny wreaths from the Pink Sleigh or other tinsel bauble decorations wired to the stocking front are very decorative. Make a yarn hanger at top before completion.

DIRECTIONS FOR TINY KNITTED BELL ORNAMENT (PLATE 60)

Two of these tied together make an exceptionally attractive lapel corsage or sell individually as ornaments.

Use No. 2 needles, and red sport yarn. Bell will be about 2 inches in length. Cast on 14 sts. For the first row, knit 10 sts. and purl the last 4. Row 2, which is the right side of your work, is made simply by knitting all the stitches. Repeat these two rows until you have 22 ridges, ending with a knit row. Bind off all stitches, and leave about a 12-inch strand of yarn after binding off the last stitch. Thread this strand of yarn into a yarn needle, and sew together the cast-on and bound-off edges. You will now be able to see a little border of stockinette stitches at one end. This is the bottom of the bell. At the other end, or top of bell, run your yarn needle through every other stitch, drawing it tight. Fasten off. Tie in a pearl clapper, or glue a jeweled clapper to a piece of yarn. New metallic yarns are also lovely with this product.

PLATE 60. Hand-knit stocking and bell ornaments; starched lace wreath ornament.

193

PLATE 61. Milkweed pods go elegant.

STARCHED LACE CHRISTMAS WREATH
(PLATE 60)

Materials required: approximately 2 yards of ¾-inch lace; can of spray starch; green spray paint; 7-inch strip of thin wire; tiny pine cones with wire stems; red and green brilliants; narrow red or green velvet ribbon; gold ornament hanging cord.

With looping motion, wind lace onto strip of wire. Bend one end so that lace does not slip off far end. Weave in and out of lace pattern according to a hole in the design so that the loops formed are of uniform size. Fill the wire very thickly with the lace. When it is quite full, cut off the lace, and forming wire into circle or wreath, clamp ends tightly, the one end secured and wound about the other. Shape loops into a graceful design. Place on sheet of cardboard, and spray with spray starch. Place in oven at 200 degrees until it dries, or in the sun or on a windowsill, or overnight. When dry, spray with bright Christmas green enamel. Repeat, when dry, turning over, so that both sides are covered. Attach tiny pine cones in three clusters, and to them strategically adhere red and green brilliants. Attach hanger. On small opening at right-bottom area of wreath, tie red or green velvet bow. Tiny pine cones are available at the Pink Sleigh.

Walnuts and milkweed pods make excellent Christmas ornaments when sprayed gold and treated with imagination. Angels, dried flowers, tiny babies, sleeping bunnies, or playful kittens all are objects which lend themselves to miniature products to sell. (See Plates 17 and 61.) The Christ Child in the walnut shell ornament is effective for Christmas sales, and a walnut half makes a fetching miniature May basket when filled with dried flowers.

THE CHRIST CHILD IN THE WALNUT
SHELL ORNAMENT (PLATE 17, PAGE 48)

This is a tremendous seller, one of the most charming ornaments that can be devised. It totally captures the spirit of Christmas. Using a nut pick, force open a whole walnut using the tiny hole, often found at the base of the shell, as a lever. It will then usually crack open in two perfect halves. Spray the two halves gold. Drill a tiny hole in back top of shell (do several dozen at a time). Attach thin gold cord for hanger. Using tiny plastic baby dolls, chosen for sweetness of expression, break off all but trunk of body, and insert remainder of doll shape, minus appendages into nutshell. With tweezers, arrange small square of wide velvet ribbon into a coverlet across baby, arranging artistically. Glue into shell, baby having been glued down beforehand. Put a proper colored small glass star on shell rim at top of baby head and three bright jewels at either sides and bottom of shell rim. Never omit the glass star, for it establishes ornament clearly as the Christ Child. Plastic babies can usually be found at party and novelty supply stores for about 10 or 15 cents each. The glass stars (flat-backed) are available at the Pink Sleigh.

For an Easter or May basket, put a tiny arrangement of straw flowers set in clay or Plastitak (a reusable adhesive manufactured by Brooks Manufacturing Company, Box 41195, Cincinnati, Ohio 45241) in your walnut half.

Acorns with their little hats, smiling faces added, make a Christmas Choir when mounted on slices of wood cut from a fallen tree branch. Owls fashioned from rounded stones and glued to driftwood or stained branches cut to size make fetching products. (See Plates 15 and 62.)

Rounded stones make Pebble People to decorate a shelf or charm a collector; ours came from the Connecticut River, and Jones Beach at Long Island, New York, is a wonderful spot for collecting pebbles of promising shapes and sizes. Epoxy glue is the strong variety of adherent required for such projects. (See Plate 63.) Knitted cap directions are at end of Chapter IV.

From upholstery webbing one can devise additional products to sell, such as the famous decorated handbags, always strong sellers. In addition, the handle measurements make a perfect matching case for glasses and the single strip of embroidered webbing, turned in at each side length, makes an attractive matching belt, a product teen-agers love.

PLATE 62. Owls on driftwood require few materials.

PLATE 63.   Pebble People tax our ingenuity and sell briskly. Popsicle sticks make skis, and toothpicks are ski poles. Bits of felt make ears, tails, and gloves. Beads and sequins make good eyes.

A brightly colored fold-up yardstick from the dime store may also be slipped into a pocket made and embroidered onto a 31-inch strip of webbing, sewn together at the sides and a pot holder hanger added to the top. (See Chapter X for where to purchase supplies.)

New containers or old containers recycled offer endless possibilities for bazaar products to sell. Cases in point are decorations made from the new plastic pillboxes, sold in every color at minimal cost per unit. We mounted ours on painted blocks of wood, presanded and sprayed, setting a miniature scene within.

A beautiful blue tree star (velvet) was decorated with the fragile Belgian glass hair-conditioner bottles* found at most beauty shops (which were happy to collect them for us). The inside of each icicle-shaped bottle was threaded with a slim thread of connected silver sequins, bought by the yard. A glued-on paper cup at the back of the ornament gives it perfect placement on the top branch of the family Christmas tree.

An extremely new and fascinating ornament may be fashioned from discarded computer tape rings (from the local telephone company or a bank), and they are new developments of the computer age. They come in yellow, green, blue, red, and ivory plastic disks. They look very much like a shiny plastic rubber mason jar top, even to the pull-out rounded handle which makes a natural hanger for the ornament. They are fairly large and showy, and a tree covered with them is spectacular. I used two together, glued back to back, with a piece of transparent thick cellophane from a Christmas card cut to size in the center, as a surface against which I could glue a scene. (Kresge stores sell this clear plastic by the yard). Scene ideas are endless. There is a Japanese-made crèche scene, fully painted, of small plastic figures which sells, bagged, at the Pink Sleigh for 10 cents a package. We put gold beading in the outside recess. Pearl beading or simple gold cord works equally well. (See Plate 64.)

A good example of a product which can be altered with little effort and thus create a new product, is a decorated flyswatter. With different dress, it is a household Christmas product. For a

* See Chapter X, Recycled or Ecological Products to make.

spring bazaar, decorate its felt sheath with a bright butterfly overlay where the Christmas tree had been in the wintertime product. Many items can be switched to summer usefulness simply by changing decoration and color scheme. Year-round sales are possible because it is a useful, practical idea. The basic flyswatter sells for 19 cents at the dime store but, decorated, it will bring 75 cents or $1 at a bazaar.

I vividly recall that at one money-raising function in which I was a willing worker, our organization was the recipient of a donation of sample perfume vials from a local cosmetic manufacturer. The perfume, we all agreed, was not particularly appealing. In fact, devastating remarks were muttered about the quality of the product. Eventually someone came up with the idea of making stuffed skunks cut from a large remnant of black and white pile fabric (the pattern procured from a child's coloring book); to these toys we tied the sample vials of perfume as nosegays at the necks of the skunks, and they proved a great sensation, selling quickly (see Plate 65).

When all imagination fails while you are attempting to turn some handout of dubious merit into a positive sale, *do* remain undaunted. Every self-respecting suburbanite housewife who ever held or attended a garage sale knows that a tableful of dust-catching objects displayed with a sign reading "Disaster!" can conceivably bring in more proceeds than a tableful of products served up with loving care.

FESTOONED FLYSWATTER

Materials required: one dime-store wire mesh flyswatter; pieces of felt in various colors (see suggestions in directions below); sequins in coordinating colors; Sobo glue; tiny gold bow sequins, if flyswatter is to be sold at Christmas.

Every household needs a flyswatter. For Easter sales the felt covers with the butterfly overlay are effective in blues and greens, oranges and yellows, pinks and purples. Common kitchen colors are good, for that's where flyswatters generally reside. For Christmas sales (the pleasing colors do not show in the picture), the Christmas tree is of hot pink felt decorating an apple green felt

PLATE 64.   The computer tape ring ornament.

PLATE 65.   A perfume sample and a sense of humor help merchandise a toy stuffed skunk.

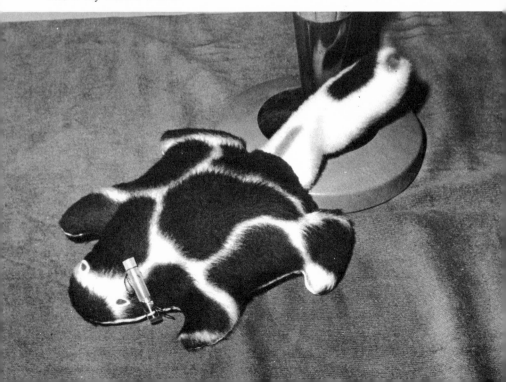

PATTERN FOR THE
FLY SWATTER

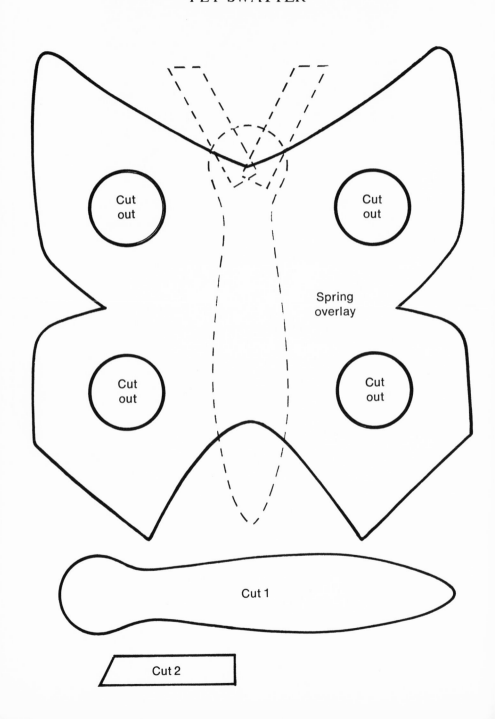

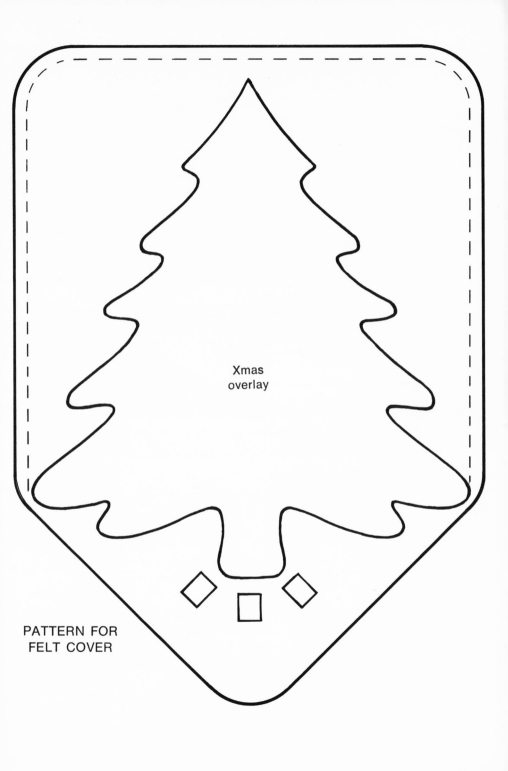

Xmas
overlay

PATTERN FOR
FELT COVER

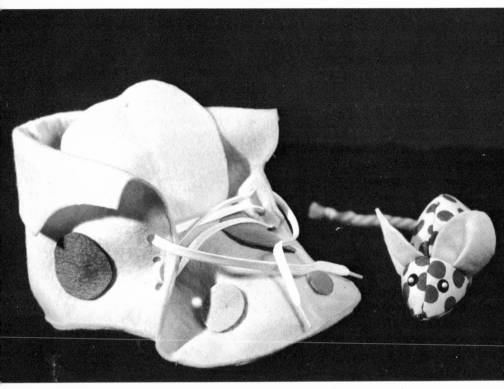

PLATE 66.   A felt boot made to hold an empty coffee tin container.

cover. Cut front and back covers of light green felt and stitch around pattern edges with hot pink thread. Glue on Christmas tree with felt ball ornaments and sequins, the felt balls cut with paper punch for uniformity of shape. Rectangular boxes cut from felt make little packages under the tree. Gilt precut bows are from the Pink Sleigh.

One of the best ideas for its versatility which comes to mind is the Santa boot, designed to fit around a coffee tin, to serve as a decorative container. Cut of red felt and decorated with white pile about the top, it helps sell nuts in bulk, hard candies, or TV mixes at Christmas. Accompanied by a black and white checked gingham mouse, it finishes the Christmas setting for every household tree. Equally fetching for spring sales, the same boot becomes the domicile for the Old Woman in the Shoe, tiny plastic babies glued to black felt cut out windows. Displayed on Easter cellophane grass, the same shoe becomes the Green Giant's left-behind footgear, along with stuffed animals in the meadow, an elf or leprechaun perched on the toe. Many liberties may be taken with a good product. (See Plate 66.)

A variation on the Santa boot might be a sewn Western boot for hanging at the chimney or a patchwork calico stocking to match the calico ornaments. Stockings designed to look like high-button Gay Nineties shoes are another suggestion, if they lend themselves better to the theme of your bazaar. (See Western Boots for Christmas, Chapter X).

In the final chapter of this book are some hints on where to go to develop the theme for your fund-raising event. The stakes are enormous, and the fellowship is enjoyable and rewarding. The most important ingredient for success is always your own enthusiasm! So go to it—you're the chairman!

PLATE 67. Russian hand-decorated Easter eggs on display. See Chapter X for purchasing information.

IX

WHAT'S FOR NEXT YEAR?

The bazaar is over, and the proceeds are in. Your achievements as a group have been loudly proclaimed and your final goals appear to be realized. However, before you take that well-earned rest, make one final effort to leave for those who come after you a clearly defined next-time starting point in the form of an assessment of all that has transpired.

To begin with, an informal talent file on your membership would be of extreme value to your successor. Some workers may have voiced an interest in a future idea which might be explored. It may have occurred to you midway in last year's bazaar that a certain type of theme would have been immensely appropriate for your organization, and you may have wished you had thought of it earlier. Jot down these suggestions in a good concise statement, and place it in your file for future chairmen.

Be sure to save copies of the timeless patterns for which there is always a market in any future undertaking: the Thanksgiving turkey, the stuffed Santa, good stuffed animals, products with year-round appeal. One of the best examples of such a product is the gay miniature man's waistcoat sold to hang onto the neck of a bottle of wine as a gift to a host or hostess the year round, particularly apropos for the holidays. It lends a personal touch to an impersonal but always welcome gift, and is timelessly popular.

WINE BOTTLE VEST

Materials required: red, black and white felt; round brass

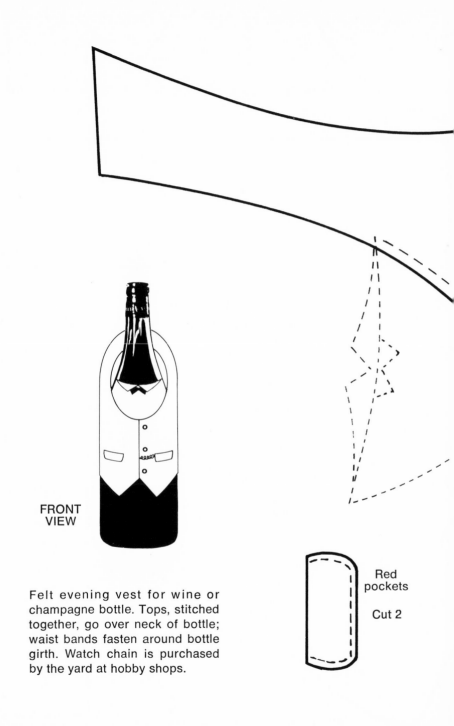

FRONT VIEW

Felt evening vest for wine or champagne bottle. Tops, stitched together, go over neck of bottle; waist bands fasten around bottle girth. Watch chain is purchased by the yard at hobby shops.

Red pockets

Cut 2

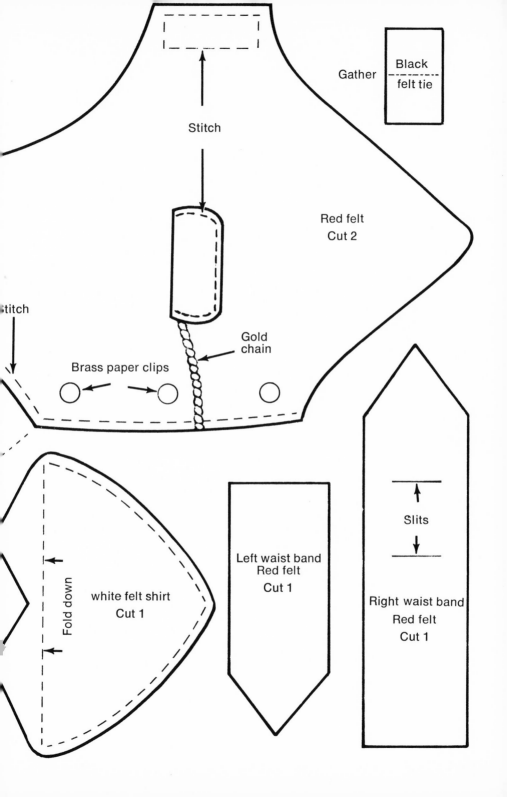

paper fasteners; "gold" watch chain (available by the yard at hobby shops).

Cut vest pieces. Stitch on waistbands and pockets. Stitch the sides of the vest together at the center seam. Insert the white shirt, and stitch down. Tack the watch chain into both pockets. Add bow tie.

Tops, stitched together, go over neck of bottle; waistbands fasten around the bottle girth.

A trend which was previously very successful but which one chairman was alert enough to recommend be discontinued, was the secondhand hat bar at a spring bazaar. Formerly, it had been one of the most productive money-makers; the following year, *no one* wore hats, and it was, appropriately enough, completely eliminated. The trend had been spotted and anticipated by a thorough, alert chairman. Today, of course, hat interest is back into full swing—especially the floppy hand-sewn, knitted, or crocheted varieties.

By trial and error, I have learned that the time to sell plants in large amounts is in November. At spring and Easter too many of the products you will offer compete for the same spot in the home; whether for decoration or for the center of the table. Therefore, fresh plants must compete with all your other products. This is not true in the fall. What growing things a household sports must then be brought indoors and what is left outdoors cannot compete with *your* offerings. Be sure to put a knowledgeable gardener or horticulturist in charge of such a booth or table.

Does someone in your area have an egg collection? Perhaps next year she would allow it to be used for public display. (See Plate 67.) Or perhaps someone has a china collection of fine old teacups and saucers which could be turned into a holiday table arrangement (women never tire of viewing such a display).

A simple file of correspondence will also save much time and effort for another year. Such a file will also help you evaluate in retrospect different booths and activities at a bazaar. Some may not prove to pay their way adequately enough to be worth continuing. This type of evaluation can be accomplished in one short meeting with individuals who shared responsibility. Real frankness is very likely to surface at a post-bazaar evaluation.

A recipe file is not a bad idea either, particularly if food items of special quality were associated with your bazaar. Here is a good place to attempt to spot trends as you look‹toward the future. America's penchant for gourmet cooking, health foods, endless cookbooks, infatuation with herbs and spices is a continuing trend which has surefire potential for future exploration. It is so all-encompassing that it is not likely to die down in a year or so. There are endless possibilities for parlaying recipes, along with products, into real profits, and I have included some in this chapter that have worked well for me. Strange, weird, eccentric, kooky, or mysterious recipes are often attention getters for women customers. They may be mimeographed into booklet form and sold for a quarter, or they may be attached to and sold as part of a product.

For example, fruit- or vegetable-shaped Christmas ornaments or pillows or pincushions could be sold alongside recipes for *Tomato* Soup Cake (*very* good), *Sauerkraut* Surprise Cake, Mashed-*potato* Cake, or other unusual combinations.

With floral products (pillows, ornaments, paper and porcelain-ized flowers, etc.) such unusual recipes as Nasturtium Salad. Calendula Dip, Nasturtium Mayonnaise, Chrysanthemum Soup, Marigold Rice, etc., might be offered. Candied mint, violets, or pecans are attention getters.

Along with sachets or herb cuttings, recipes for Dry-Rose Potpourri, Moist-Rose Potpourri, Marigold and Mint Potpourri, Country Herb, Lavender Jar, or Spice Potpourris are fitting. Products to make for sale from these scents are closet bags (6-inch checked gingham pastel cotton bags with pinked edges, tied with a satin bow for hanging), or large square patchwork sachets (4 inches square) made of velvet, satin, or brocade, calicos or soft delicate materials. The Potpourri Shop in Redding Ridge, Connecticut,* sells six cups of do-it-yourself bulk mix

* See Chapter X.

in "Old-Fashioned Rose," Country Spice, or Lemon-Herb fragrances.

Other products such as pomander balls, quilted calico bags with solid color lining used as scented drawer bags, tea cozies, or pot holders for kitchen drawers are good ideas. A 35-cent *Primer for Herb Gardening* is available from the Herb Society of America.

The recipe for salt and flour ornaments to make at home or for sugar mold ornaments are another idea, particularly if you also have some of the finished product to sell.

Spice Combinations

SEVENTEENTH-CENTURY SPICY SACHET RECIPE

1 tonka bean
2 ounces dry rose petals
2 ounces lavender flowers
1 ounce orrisroot
2 tablespoons cloves
2 tablespoons cinnamon

Grate tonka bean over remaining ingredients; mix and keep in closed container for two weeks to blend.

DRY ROSE POTPOURRI

1 quart dried rose petals
¼ to ½ cup dried rose buds (damask roses work well)
1 ounce orris powder
1 tablespoon ground mace
2 tablespoons whole cloves
1 vanilla bean, cut or broken into small pieces
1 tablespoon cardamon in pods, crushed
2 sticks cinnamon, crushed
20 drops oil of orange or 10 drops each
    oil of lemon and oil of orange

NOTE: Never use oils found in the supermarkets for a potpourri as these are almost certain to contain undesirable additives. Oils for potpourris may be purchased from the Potpourri Shop, previously mentioned (see Chapter X for address).

Combine dried rose petals and rose buds with orris. Lightly mix with hands or wooden fork and spoon in a large bowl. Blend mace, cloves, vanilla bean, cardamon and cinnamon separately. Add to rose mix. Blend well. Drop orange (or orange and lemon) oil over mix; stir gently. Place in jars with tight-fitting lids (or in double plastic bags, each bag sealed with the twisters). Store unopened for six weeks, shaking often. When ready to use, place in a pretty container. Stir gently; a rich fragrance will rise.

MOIST ROSE POTPOURRI

2 quarts rose petals, fresh, fragrant varieties— pick in the morning
Coarse kosher-type salt (do *not* use iodized salt)
2 ounces orris powder
¼ ounce mace
¼ ounce ground cloves
1 small stick cinnamon, crushed
¼ ounce ground nutmeg
¼ ounce ground allspice
5 drops oil of rose or oil of jasmine

Gather freshly opened, unbruised petals in a variety of colors. Spread out on paper toweling and let dry till they lose about half their bulk and have a leathery, half-dry look. Place in large jars or crocks with lids, layering roses with salt. Continue alternating layers of roses and salt, ending with salt, only until container is two-thirds full. Cover tightly, and store away from heat and light for three weeks. (If a liquid forms, press down petals with the back of a spoon and pour off residual liquid.) After three weeks, remove from jars. Shake away salt. If petals have caked together, flake lightly with fingers. Place petals in a large bowl. Mix orris and all spices together separately and add to roses. Return to jars with tight-fitting lids. Store unopened for six weeks. When ready to use, add oil gradually, stirring gently.

MARIGOLD AND MINT POTPOURRI

1 cup leaf thyme
1¼ cups whole peppermint leaves
¾ cup leaf basil
1 cup coarse salt
1 cup dried marigold flowers

Blend the herbs and salt carefully, being careful not to crush the herbs. Mix in marigolds. Ripen and store as in Country Herb Potpourri.

COUNTRY HERB POTPOURRI

¼ cup dried lemon peel
¼ cup dried orange peel
¼ cup dried lime peel
1 cup leaf marjoram
1½ cups leaf rosemary
½ cup leaf sage
1 or 2 bay leaves, coarsely broken
¼ cup summer savory
1 cup coarse salt

To prepare your peels, pare fruits with a vegetable parer; try not to pick up the white pith. Spread the strips of peel on a plate to dry thoroughly. Break them up coarsely; measure out desired amounts. The bright yellow, orange, and green peels will add color to the potpourri, in addition to the citrus scent. Blend the herbs and peels together in a big bowl. Mix with hands or wooden spoons, and crush the herbs very slightly. Add the salt and mix thoroughly. Let "ripen" in jars with tight-fitting lids, away from light and heat, for four to six weeks; then place in decorative jar with a tight-fitting lid. When ready to use, open jar, stir potpourri gently, and leave the cover off for a while. If you want a strong citrus scent, you may increase the amount of peel.

LAVENDER JAR POTPOURRI

1 cup lavender leaves
2 cups lemon verbena leaves
1 cup dried carnation petals (optional)
1 cup any dried white flowers and petals
1 ounce orris powder

Blend flowers and leaves in a bowl with hands or wooden fork. Sprinkle on orris. Mix gently. Store in jars with tight-fitting lids for a month, away from heat and light, shaking from time to time. Then place in decorative jars; open and stir gently to use.

SPICE POTPOURRI

1 tablespoon anise seed, crushed
1 tablespoon whole allspice, crushed
5 or 6 nutmegs, coarsely broken
1 teaspoon powdered ginger (optional)
4 or 5 sticks cinnamon, coarsely broken
¼ cup whole cloves
½ teaspoon ground cinnamon
2 or 3 whole vanilla beans,
    cut or broken into small pieces
1 cup coarse salt

Perhaps the easiest way to crush the small pieces is with a mortar or pestle. The nutmegs should be broken with a hammer or on carving board. Mix all the spices carefully together; add the salt. Mix thoroughly. Ripen and store as in Country Herb Potpourri. This potpourri has a wonderfully exotic scent without being heavy or overpowering and is particularly appropriate for a man's room or closet.

Unusual Recipes Pertinent to Flowers

NASTURTIUM SALAD

Young nasturtium leaves have a cresslike flavor and, with

tender nasturtium blossoms as a garnish, make an elegant salad. Blossoms and leaves are edible.

12 young nasturtium leaves
4 young nasturtium blossoms
1 small head Bibb or Boston lettuce
1 clove garlic
Roquefort or blue cheese dressing

Wash and let dry nasturtium leaves, blossoms, and lettuce. Mince garlic finely into salad bowl, and cover with dressing. Just before you are ready to serve the salad, mix in nasturtium leaves, torn, and lettuce leaves, coating well with dressing. Garnish with blossoms, and serve one blossom with each portion. Serves 4.

CALENDULA SPICE

Pick 2 cups calendula flowers. Strip off petals, spread on a cookie sheet, and dry in oven at low until crackling. Crumble and store in an herb jar, tightly sealed and away from the light. Use to color and flavor mashed potatoes, noodles, cream sauces, custards and cornstarch desserts.

CALENDULA DIP

18-ounce package cream cheese
½ stick butter
3 tablespoons cream or milk
2 teaspoons dried calendula spice (see above)
1 teaspoon snipped fresh dill
2 pickle rounds
Fresh calendula petals
Sprig fresh dillweed

In mixer, whip cream cheese, butter and cream or milk with calendula spice until smooth. Beat in dill snips. Turn into wide shallow dip dish, and smooth the top. Decorate with a pickle posy, using pickle rounds as flower head, fresh calendula for petals, and a dill sprig as the stem.

216

CHRYSANTHEMUM SOUP

2 cans chicken consommé
1 small can water chestnuts, sliced
Tops of 2 scallions, thinly sliced
Peel of 1 lemon, thinly slivered
2 slices cold boiled ham, shredded
1 large fresh chrysanthemum
6 sprigs parsley
Soy sauce

Heat consommé to boiling point, but do not boil. Add water chestnuts, green tops of scallions, ham, and lemon peel. Remove petals from chrysanthemum, wash, drain, and add to soup. Bring to a boil, and serve at once with garnish of parsley and a dash of soy sauce in each bowl. Serves 4 to 6.

NASTURTIUM MAYONNAISE

Depending on the intensity of the color of the blossoms used, this makes a decorative dressing for hearts of lettuce, sliced tomatoes, cucumber salad or avocado stuffed with crabmeat.

½ pint mayonnaise
24 nasturtium blossoms
2 tablespoons heavy cream

Place all ingredients in an electric blender, and whirl at high speed for 1 minute. Place in jar, and store in refrigerator until ready for use. Make slightly more than ½ pint.

MARIGOLD RICE

3 cups chicken or beef bouillon
3 cups instant rice
1 medium onion, sautéed in butter
½ teaspoon rosemary
3 teaspoons dried marigold petals

Bring bouillon to a boil, add all other ingredients, turn off heat, and cover tightly. Allow to stand for 15 minutes. Stir with a fork and serve. Serves 6.

MASHED POTATO CAKE

2½ cups all-purpose flour
¾ cups cocoa
2 teaspoons baking powder
1 teaspoon cinnamon
1 teaspoon nutmeg
1 cup butter
2 cups sugar
4 eggs, beaten
1 cup mashed potatoes
½ cup milk
1 teaspoon vanilla
1 cup broken nuts

Sift flour several times; add cocoa, baking powder and spices. Cream butter and sugar; add eggs and potatoes. Add dry ingredients alternately with milk and vanilla. Add nuts. Pour into two greased and floured 9″ cake pans. Bake at 350 degrees until tests done.

TOMATO SOUP CAKE

1 cup sugar
½ cup butter
1 teaspoon cinnamon
½ teaspoon cloves
½ teaspoon nutmeg
2 cups flour
1 teaspoon baking soda in 1 can tomato soup
1 cup raisins

Mix all ingredients except raisins well; pour into square cake pan. Bake in 350 degree oven for 45 minutes.

Frosting: 1 package cream cheese, about 1 cup confectioner's sugar, ½ teaspoon vanilla.

Soften cream cheese at room temperature. Sift in sugar. Add vanilla.

SAUERKRAUT SURPRISE CAKE

Sauerkraut adds moistness and coconutlike texture but no sour flavor.

½ cup butter or margarine
1½ cups sugar
3 eggs
1 teaspoon vanilla
2 cups sifted all-purpose flour
1 teaspoon baking powder
1 teaspoon baking soda
¼ teaspoon salt
½ cup cocoa
1 cup water
1 8-ounce can (1 cup) sauerkraut,
    drained, rinsed, and finely snipped

In large mixing bowl, cream butter or margarine and sugar till light. Beat in eggs, one at a time; add vanilla. Sift together flour, baking powder, soda, salt, and cocoa; add to creamed mixture alternately with water, beating after each addition. Stir in sauerkraut. Turn into greased and floured 13×9×2-inch pan. Bake in 350 degree oven for 35 to 40 minutes. Cool in pan. Frost with Sour Cream-Chocolate Frosting (below). Cut into squares to serve.

SOUR CREAM-CHOCOLATE FROSTING

Melt 1 6-ounce package semisweet chocolate pieces and 4 tablespoons butter or margarine over low heat. Remove from heat; blend in ½ cup dairy sour cream, 1 teaspoon vanilla, and ¼ teaspoon salt. Gradually add sifted confectioner's sugar (2½ to 2¾ cups) to make spreading consistency. Beat well.

PUMPKIN CAKE

1¾ cups all-purpose flour
2 teaspoons baking powder
1 teaspoon baking soda

1 teaspoon salt
2 teaspoons cinnamon
½ teaspoon nutmeg
¼ teaspoon allspice
¼ teaspoon ginger or
   1 tablespoon pie spice
⅔ cup buttermilk or sour milk
½ cup shortening
1⅓ cups sugar
2 eggs
1 cup cooked pumpkin

Sift dry ingredients. Cream shortening and sugar, add eggs, and beat. In separate bowl, combine pumpkin and buttermilk; add with flour to creamed mixture. Bake in 9 inch pan, paper-lined and greased, at 350 degrees for 45 minutes. Center *must* spring back. (Delicious with a white butter frosting.)

Kookie Recipes (Really Different)

JELLO CANDY

3 cups sugar
¾ cup light corn syrup
¾ cup water
2 egg whites
1 package flavored gelatine

Boil sugar, syrup and water till it will string or spin a thread. Beat the egg whites stiff; add the gelatine and beat it in. Pour the boiled syrup over the egg whites mixture, and beat until stiff. Drop by teaspoonsful onto waxed paper to cool.

DOUGHNUT CUPCAKES

⅓ cup soft shortening
1 cup sugar
1 egg, beaten
½ cup milk

1½ cups all-purpose flour
1½ teaspoons baking powder
½ teaspoon salt
¼ teaspoon nutmeg
6 tablespoons melted butter
½ cup sugar
1 teaspoon cinnamon

Cream shortening and 1 cup sugar together. Add egg, milk, flour, baking powder, salt, and nutmeg; mix. Bake in muffin tins at 375 degrees for about 15 minutes. Take out at once, and roll in melted butter; then roll in ½ cup sugar and cinnamon mixed together.

SALT AND FLOUR ORNAMENTS

1 part all-purpose flour
1 part salt
A few drops of water
  (enough to make the mixture a spongy mass)
  Dry tempera paint

Mix flour, salt, and water thoroughly, and to give the mix color, add a little tempera. Cookie cutters can be used to shape ornaments. Roll thin, and cut out stars, reindeer, angels, gingerbread men, or whatever you like. Pierce a hole for string. They can be painted, glazed with shellac and trimmed with sequins and glitter after being allowed to dry for two or three days. Mounting them on colored metallic paper is another touch to help make each an original creation.

THE WORLD'S BEST SUGAR COOKIE

This is a recipe for cutout cookies which may be used for the stand-up cookies for which instructions are given in this book.*

---

* See Elephant and Bunny Stand-Up Cookies, Chapter IV; also Stained Glass Cookies (recipe follows), in which this recipe for a sugar cookie may be used.

1½ cups sugar
2 eggs, beaten
3½ cups all-purpose flour
1 cup butter
1 teaspoon vanilla
1 teaspoon baking powder
½ teaspoon salt

Cream butter; add sugar and beat. Add vanilla and eggs. Add all dry ingredients. Roll out on a well-floured board, and cut into festive shapes. Bake in hot oven (400 degrees) about 10 minutes. Makes 8 dozen small cookies.

STAINED GLASS COOKIES FOR CHRISTMAS OR EASTER BAZAARS (PLATE 16, PAGE 45)

⅓ cup shortening
⅓ cup sugar
1 egg
⅔ cup honey
1 teaspoon lemon

These should be blended together until creamy.

3 cups all-purpose flour
1 teaspoon baking soda
1 teaspoon salt

These should be sifted together and added to the sugar-shortening mixture.

Combine creamed and sifted dry ingredients. Chill. Roll out in ¼" strips, or as narrow as possible. Cookie dough is used for the "leading," and clear, brightly colored hard candy, such as sour balls or lollipops, for the "stained glass." Crush the colored candy into coarse lumps. This is easy if you put a clean cloth over the hammer. Keep each color of candy in a separate sectioned dish such as a muffin tin. Cut rolled-out, chilled dough into ¼" strips, or roll into thin ropes. Join the ends to form square, rec-

STAINED GLASS COOKIES
For Christmas *Or* Easter Bazaars

SOME SUGGESTED
COOKIE PATTERNS

1.

2.

3.

4.

Red candy
only

5.

tangular, or circular shapes for the outline of the window, as you put them on a piece of aluminum foil on a cookie sheet. Fill the crushed candy into the open spaces—a very small amount of candy, just enough to cover the spaces lightly. Bake at 350 degrees *for three to five minutes only*. Watch closely, and remove from oven when candy is just melted smooth. Chill before peeling cookies from aluminum foil.

EASTER PASHKA

Traditional dessert of old Russia.

> 4 8-ounce packages cream cheese
> 1 cup (2 sticks) butter
> 3 egg yolks
> 2 cups confectioner's sugar
> 2 teaspoons vanilla
> ¾ cup chopped citron
> ¾ cup toasted slivered almonds
> Frozen strawberries for sauce

Day before, let cream cheese, butter and egg yolks stand at room temperature for 2 hours. Beat cream cheese in mixing bowl at low speed. Add butter, then sugar, and finally egg yolks. Add vanilla, fold in citron and almonds. Let stand. Wash well and dry inside of a 2-quart clay or plastic flowerpot; it will need a hole in the bottom for drainage. Line the pot with a double thickness of cheesecloth wrung out in cold water. Spoon the cheese mixture into the pot. Cover with Saran and refrigerate overnight. To unmold, invert a dessert epergne pedestal plate over the flowerpot, and quickly turn right side up. Gently lift off pot. Remove cheesecloth slowly. Garnish the base and top with whole strawberries, perhaps upright strawberry halves all around base. Serve with a spoonful of crushed, sweetened strawberries. Serves 30 to 35, as a little goes a long way. It is deliciously rich.

EASTER HAM SAUCE

Serve hot over ham or lamb for a culinary triumph. Marvelous over slices of clove-studded baked ham!

1 bottle mint sauce
1 bottle chili sauce
    (same approximate size)
1 glass quince jelly

Heat together.

DIRECTIONS FOR HANDMADE PAPIER-MÂCHÉ POTS
FOR SMALL EASTER TREES
(SEE CHAPTER II)

You will need ready-made papier-mâché mix, gesso, (a chalky paintlike first coat sealer used before painting), and bathroom-sized dixie cups cut down about ½ inch. The mix and gesso are available at any good art store.

Grasp the cup in the left hand; this is the base to which you will adhere the moistened mix. Apply with a butter knife, smoothing as you work. Do first the inside surface, then the top (inside). After this dries in a slow oven (under 200 degrees) or overnight, do outside surfaces and bottom, inverting to dry. Paint on gesso, covering all surfaces. When this dries (quickly), you are ready to spray-paint pots with lovely pastel enamels. When dry, wind a finishing strip of braid around top, and glue it securely. Cover seam at front with matching glued-on butterfly, rosebud, or jeweled decoration for a finished look. Sparkle grass (aqua, from the Pink Sleigh) adds glamor. It is easy to make 24 at one time, using cookie sheets.

If time does not permit this handmade look and approach, a very inexpensive container for a small Easter tree could be the 2-inch plastic tulip cup sold as a nut cup by Wilton Enterprises, 6 for $1.25—Item No. 1008 A 1005, Wilton Enterprises, Inc., 833 West Fifteenth, Chicago, Illinois 60643.

* See Easter trees, small and large sizes, Chapter II, Plates 8 and 9.

X

SOURCES FOR BAZAAR SUPPLIES
AND
HOW TO ORDER ADDITIONAL
PATTERNS DESCRIBED
IN THIS BOOK

General Catalogs for Bazaar Supplies

HANDCRAFTER'S CATALOG OF CREATIVE CRAFTS
1 West Brown Street, Waupun, Wisconsin 53963.

HAZEL PEARSON HANDICRAFTS
4128 Temple City Boulevard, Rosemead, California 91770—$1.

HERB FARM
Barnard Road, Granville, Massachusetts 01034. Catalog 25 cents. Excellent ideas.

HERSCHNER'S QUALITY NEEDLECRAFT
Fred Herschner Company, Stevens Point, Wisconsin 54481. Sewing supplies, craft and bazaar items.

HOLIDAY HANDICRAFTS INC.
Winsted, Connecticut 06098. Music boxes and miniatures.

HOME-SEW INC.
Bethlehem, Pennsylvania 19018. Most inexpensive way to purchase sewing supplies.

LEE WARDS
840 North State Street, Elgin, Illinois 60120. General craft suppliers.

MAID OF SCANDINAVIA

3245 Raleigh Avenue, Minneapolis, Minnesota 55416. Catalog 50 cents. Best catalog in the business for bazaar supplies; miniatures, baking decorations, ideas, books; an invaluable source.

PINK SLEIGH

Oldwick, New Jersey 08858. Catalog, 50 cents. Largest indoor craft display center in the United States. Specializes in miniatures, jewels, braids, kits, ideas, supplies. A crafter's paradise. Pioneers in the craft business.

POTPOURRI SHOP

Box 208, Redding Ridge, Connecticut 06876. Herbs, sachets by bulk, oils, scents, spices. Ideas for products of this type to sell.

S & S ARTS AND CRAFTS

Colchester, Connecticut 06098. Boutique and craft suppliers for Easter and Christmas products.

SOURCES OF SUPPLY FOR EGGERS AND ALL CRAFTERS

Kit Stansbury, 411 Warren Street, Phillipsburg, New Jersey 08865. 75 cents for complete catalog of suppliers and shops: where to get miniatures, etc.

WILTON ENTERPRISES, INC.

833 West 115th Street, Chicago, Illinois 60643. Baking suppliers–miniatures; catalog $1.

Free Brochures (Kits, Patterns, Ideas, or All Three)

ABBEY PRESS

St. Meinrad, Indiana 47577; spring and fall brochures. Books, posters, items for bazaar decorations and resale; ideas for products. Sells 35-cent *I Like Christmas* book.

GOLDEN UNICORN

22 Rustic Drive, Howell Township, Lakewood, New Jersey 08701. Brochures of extreme fascination; unique enterprise. Pine cones, bulk wreath suppliers (dried products) for resale; discounts. Any kind of pine cone or seedpod at bulk prices.

227

IDEALS PUBLICATIONS
Bazaar Decorative Pictures; 11315 Watertown Plank Road, Milwaukee, Wisconsin 53226. Seasonal themes, group prices; books for resale.

LELAND OF RESEDA
P.O. Box 1009, Reseda, California 91335. Brochure of craft patterns to make.

NEW HAMPTON GENERAL STORE
Box 872 Hampton, New Jersey 08827.

PIONEER CRAFTS
P.O. Box 8, Cedar Grove, New Jersey 07009. Craft projects suitable for bazaars; kits and patterns.

VERMONT COUNTRY STORE
Weston, Vermont 05161. Real American calico, 89 cents a yard. Sample swatches. Authentic.

Sources for Bazaar Ideas

BAZAAR BEST SELLERS
Woman's Day, September, 1968; 50 cents. Write Box 1000, Greenwich, Connecticut 06830.

BAZAAR GIFTS TO MAKE
Good Housekeeping Booklet Number 801 *Loving Gifts to Make for Special People*; 75 cents; Good Housekeeping Bulletin Service, 959 Eighth Avenue, New York, New York 10019.

BAZAAR PRODUCTS (EASTER)
Holiday Sewing magazine—$1, January, 1973—pages 40–41; also "Terry-Toys" same issue; write Countrywide Publications, 222 Park Avenue South, New York, New York 1003.

BLUE RIDGE HEARTHSIDE CRAFTS
P.O. Box 96, Sugar Grove, North Carolina 28679. Free brochure. Excellent source for ideas for handmade crafts and products.

CATALOG OF AMERICAN HANDICRAFTS
Department 10, 1655 Wisconsin Avenue, Washington, D.C. 20007.

CLYMER'S OF BUCKS COUNTY
Chestnut Street, Nashua, New Hampshire 03060. Ideas for products.

FARM JOURNAL CHRISTMAS BOOKS, 1971 AND 1972
Edited by Kathryn Larson; $5.95; Doubleday & Co., Garden City, New York 11530. Products and recipes.

FOLK TOYS AROUND THE WORLD AND HOW TO MAKE THEM
Item No. 5016; $3.50; United States Committee for UNICEF, P.O. Box 5050, New York, New York 10017.

GRANDMOTHER'S SOFT TOY SHOP
P.O. Box 39, Fabyan, Connecticut 06245. Most unusual soft toy products. 20 cents for brochure.

HANDMADE FROM A BROOKLYN BROWNSTONE
25 cents; Brownstone Gifts, 108 Pierrepont Street, Brooklyn, New York 11201.

HERB FARM
Barnard Road, Granville, Massachusetts 01034. 25 cents; ideas for products and items for resale.

HARRIET CARTER CATALOG
Write Department 22, Plymouth Meeting, Pennsylvania 19462. Ideas.

HOMESPUN PRODUCTS USA
Route 1, Gastonia, North Carolina 28052

"AN OLD-FASHIONED CHRISTMAS"—book
By Paul Engle; Dial Press, 730 Third Avenue, New York, New York 10017. $3.95; stories, poems, themes, ideas for authentic products to make for an old-fashioned Christmas. Excellent.

THE POTPOURRI SHOP
Redding Ridge, Connecticut 06876. Sachets and spices sold by bulk to make products for resale. Catalog.

SHOPPING INTERNATIONAL
Norwich, Vermont 05055. Free brochure. Easter, Christmas toys and ideas.

SLEEPY HOLLOW GIFTS
6651 Arlington Boulevard, Falls Church, Virginia 22042. Ideas.

"TREES OF CHRISTMAS"—book
By Edna Metcalfe; Abingdon Press, Nashville, Tennessee 37219; under $10. Trees from all over the world with directions for duplication of ornaments. Excellent source for products to make.

1225 SHOP
745 Alexander Road, Princeton, New Jersey 07009. Crafted projects suitable for bazaars; idea-stimulating. Christmas brochure contains unusual holiday recipes to use.

Useful Magazines for Idea Sources

BETTER HOMES AND GARDENS
Meredith Corporation, 1716 Locust Street, Des Moines, Iowa 50336.

CREATIVE CRAFTS
31 Arch Street, Ramsey, New Jersey 07746.

FAMILY CIRCLE AND FAMILY CIRCLE SPECIAL
CHRISTMAS PROJECTS BOOKS
488 Madison Avenue, New York, New York 10022.

FASHION AND NEEDLECRAFT IDEAS
Conso Publishing Company, 149 Fifth Avenue, New York, New York 10010.

GOLDEN HANDS
6 Commercial Street, Hicksville, New York 11801.

GOOD HOUSEKEEPING
959 Eighth Avenue, New York, New York 10019.

LADY'S CIRCLE AND LADY'S CIRCLE 1,001 CHRISTMAS IDEAS
21 West Twenty-Sixth Street, New York, New York 10010.

MC CALL'S AND MC CALL'S NEEDLEWORK AND CRAFT
MAGAZINES; ANNUALS OF CREATIVE HANDICRAFTS
230 Park Avenue, New York, New York 10017
PACK-O-FUN
14 Main Street, Park Ridge, Illinois 60068.

POPULAR CRAFTS
Published bimonthly—$1. Challenge Publications, 7950 Deering
Avenue, Canoga Park, California 91304.

POPULAR HANDICRAFTS AND HOBBIES
Tower Press, P.O. Box 428, Seabrook, New Hampshire 03874.

STITCH AND SEW
Tower Press. P.O. Box 428, Seabrook, New Hampshire 03874.

WOMAN'S DAY AND WOMAN'S DAY SPECIAL
CHRISTMAS PROJECTS BOOKS
Fawcett Publications, Greenwich, Connecticut 06830.

Specialized Sources of Information for Mounting a Bazaar
(Aids To Make Your Bazaar an Event of Distinction)

BUTTONS
Unusual; for bazaar sewing (ladybug, white mouse, hare and
turtle), House of York, 63 Oak Leaf Drive, Doylestown Pennsylvania 18901.

CAKE HOUSE (Table Decoration)
By Wyoma C. Baley; 50 cents; write Maid of Scandinavia, 3245
Raleigh Avenue, Minneapolis, Minnesota 55416.

CHRISTMAS POEMS FOR POSTERS AND DECORATION
Hormel Ham Ad—December, 1972 *Family Circle*, page 121,
488 Madison Avenue, New York, New York 10022.

CHRISTMAS POEMS (SUITABLE FOR BAZAAR USE)
Any Christmas editions of *Ideals* magazine; $1.75; Ideals Publications, 11315 Watertown Plank Road, Milwaukee, Wisconsin 53226.

CHRISTMAS TREE DECORATION
Smashing decorations for show-stopping bazaar decoration. The ultimate in Christmas tree lighting: twinkling star lights created by hundreds of crystal clear light fibers (space age lighting miracle). Sprays contain no electricity; each set has 15 miniature replaceable bulbs, each working independently. 15 indoor lights, $7.95; 15 outdoor, $9.95. Matching snowball treetop star with light fibers, $8.95. Write The Gourmet Pantry, 400 McGuiness Boulevard; Brooklyn, New York 11222. Items number 200, 210, and 201 respectively.

"COOKIE ANIMALS FOR SHOW—
HOW TO BAKE AND BUILD SAME"
By Wyoma C. Bailey, $1.55; Item Number 90824, Maid of Scandinavia Catalog, 3245 Raleigh Avenue, Minneapolis, Minnesota 55416.

COOKIE CUTTER TREE FOR DISPLAY
Woman's Day, December, 1972, page 64; Fawcett Publications, Greenwich, Connecticut 06830.

COOKIE CUTTER WREATH FOR DISPLAY
Family Circle for December, 1972, page 42. 488 Madison Avenue, New York, New York 10022.

COOKIE CUTTERS (VERY UNUSUAL)
Model Train; Cookie Village; Museum-Piece, etc.—write Fox Run Craftsmen, Huntingdon Valley, ·Pennsylvania 19006. Or write Miles Kimball, Oshkosh, Wisconsin 54901. Village set, $2 item number 7142.

COOKIES, STAINED GLASS
This book, Chapter IX. See Plate 16, page 45.

COOKIES, STAND-UP
Chapter IV, this book. Recipe: Chapter IX.

232

COOKIES, STAR-BRIGHT OR "MAGIC WINDOW"
"Fashion a Tree of Star-Bright Cookies," pages 56 and 154, *Family Circle*, December, 1972; 488 Madison Avenue, New York, New York 10022.

DISNEYLAND SUGAR MOLDS
Wilton Enterprises Catalog, 833 West 115th, Chicago, Illinois 60643.

EASTER EGGS, CZECH-HAND-DECORATED
Item number 5030, 12 at $5.95; Shopping International, Norwich, Vermont 05055.

EASTER EGGS, HAND-DECORATED, CLAY AND WOODEN
See Plate 67, this book. Created by the late Mr. Alexander Afanasieff, obtainable while they last at St. Nicholas Russian Cathedral, 15 East Ninety-seventh Street, New York, New York 10029. Truly beautiful and authentic.

EASTER EGGS, HAND-PAINTED, LIGHTED, AND STRUNG
For smashing bazaar easter egg tree. See Plate 11, this book. Item number 8284A2, Helen Gallagher Foster House, 6523 North Galena Road, Peoria, Illinois 61614.

EASTER INFORMATION AND IDEAS
For posters or giveaway books to bazaar public, see "Has Easter Laid an Egg?" by J. J. Leary, *Coronet* magazine, 50 cents, April, 1972. (Coronet Communications, 315 Park Avenue South, New York, New York 10010.)

EASTER OR SPRING BAZAAR DECORATIONS
Directions for Wind Swingers (turtle, butterfly, fish, chick, snail, caterpillar, and other simple animal mobiles). *McCall's Annual of Creative Hand-Crafts*, Volume 3, pages 97, 98, and 116; $1.20. McCall's Pattern Company, 230 Park Avenue, New York, New York 10017.

EASTER TABLECLOTH (FOR USE ON EASTER DISPLAY TABLE)
Use Martex sheet pattern "Counting Sheep" in green and white; B. Altman & Company, New York, New York; or daffodil pattern

called "Innisfree" by Martex. Also numerous tulip patterns now available.

ECOLOGY CRAFTS

Ideas for ecological bazaar—page 60, *Better Homes And Gardens Crafts And Sewing*, $1.35 (1972). Meredith Corporation, 1716 Locust Street, Des Moines, Iowa 50336. See Plate 48, this book. Also many products in Chapter VIII.

EGG CUPS (TULIP SHAPE)

For tiny plants or to sell with egg cozy, Maid of Scandinavia Catalog, item number 91995, 4 to a set, $2. 3245 Raleigh Avenue, Minneapolis, Minnesota 55416.

EQUIPMENT, BAZAAR

1. FOOD DECORATION

   Maid of Scandinavia Catalog, 3245 Raleigh Avenue, Minneapolis, Minnesota 55416.

2. PAPER OVERSEAS CAPS FOR ADVERTISING

   Mount Ellis Paper Company, Newburgh, New York 12550.

3. PHOTO BUTTONS

   Of your church or bazaar-site. For resale; photo not returnable. MAR Enterprises, 628 South Seventh Street, Lindenhurst, New York 11757.

4. POSTER PAINTING

   For bazaars. Page 24, *Popular Handicrafts and Hobbies*, December–January, 1973. Tower Press, Box 428, Seabrook, New Hampshire 13874.

   POSTER DECORATIONS

   "Olde English" Decorations from Hazel Pearson Handicrafts line of art print originals by Anton Pieck. Local craft or hobby shops, or write Hazel Pearson Handicrafts, 4128 Temple City Boulevard, Rosemead, California 91770.

5. PROGRAM HELPS IN CONJUNCTION WITH MINI-BAZAARS

   New program ideas—eight-page booklet *A Church Herald Meeting Plan and Kit*. Write the Church Herald, 630 Myrtle Street, North West, Grand Rapids, Michigan 49504.

Of exceptional brilliance, for "boutiqueing"—Westchester Hobby Shop, 102 East Post Road, White Plains, New York 10601.

HOUSE CENTERPIECE
For theme use in many bazaar plans. *Fashion and Needlecraft Ideas*, Spring/Summer, 1972, page 64; Book Number 2, 75 cents. Conso Publishing Company, 149 Fifth Avenue, New York, New York 10010.

JEWISH FESTIVAL COOKING
Bazaar helps for Jewish groups. Festival of Lights, etc. See "Festival Cooking Everyone Loves," *Family Circle,* December, 1972, page 98; 488 Madison Avenue, New York, New York 10022.

LABELS
For marking bazaar products with your group's name: small picture such as bird, Christmas tree, flag, pine tree, cactus etc. 500 for $2, 20 letters per line, 4 lines. Bruce Bolind, 1811 Bolind Building, Boulder, Colorado 80302.

NOAH'S ARK
And all the animals. Fabulous bazaar centerpiece and decoration; pattern and all directions; $1.25. Ladies' Home Journal, Dept. FCT, 641 Lexington Avenue, New York, New York 10022. See Plate 35.

OLD-FASHIONED BOOKS TO LOOK AT AND TO SELL
1. 1904 GOLD-MEDAL FLOUR COOKBOOK
2. 1890 REPRINT OF "NIGHT BEFORE CHRISTMAS"
3. CHRISTMAS DELIGHTS: 1885
4. SANTA CLAUS AND HIS WORKS: 1870
5. AN OLD-FASHIONED CHRISTMAS IN PICTURES

All these are available at $1 to $2 from Federal Small-wares, 85 Fifth Avenue, New York, New York 10003, or from Miles Kimball, Oshkosh, Wisconsin 54901; items 1, 2, 3, 4 are listed by Kimball as numbers 7069, 9640, 9993, and 9996 respectively.

Doll House type. For display or to sell. *Better Homes and Gardens Crafts and Sewing, 1972*; $1.35; page 95; Meredith Corporation, 1716 Locust Street, Des Moines, Iowa 50336.

WEBBING HANDBAGS
To make and sell. Upholstery webbing kits, Pioneer Crafts, Box 8, Cedar Grove, New Jersey 07009.
Also The Stitchery, 204 Worcester Turnpike, Wellesley Hills, Massachusetts 02181; also Fred Herschner & Company, Stevens Point, Wisconsin 54481. 72-yard rolls of webbing, $16.50 plus tax, Barclay Hardware, Pleasantville, New York 10570.

WILLIAMSBURG CHRISTMAS
Theme for bazaar. Feel of colonial days. See *Christmas in Williamsburg* or *Christmas in New England*, both by Taylor Biggs Lewis, Jr., and Joanne B. Young; $4.95 and $5.95 respectively; Rinehart and Winston, Inc. New York, New York.

Products Described in Chapter I

STRAWBERRY FESTIVAL
  APRON WITH STRAWBERRIES AND FRUIT
  Apron, McCall Pattern Number 3063, 85 cents; *Strawberry and Fruit*, Claudia Iron-Ons, Claudia Designs Inc., 364 Adam Street, Bedford Hills, New York 10507; photo in *Seventeen Magazine's Make It*, Fall/Winter, 1972; $1; Triangle Communications, 320 Park Avenue, New York, New York 10022.
  STRAWBERRY RECIPES
  Woman's Day and *Family Circle*, May, 1972, Issues.
  STRAWBERRY SHOW-OFFS (Ideas)
  Better Homes and Gardens, May, 1972.
  STRAWBERRY FESTIVAL (Ideas)
  Ladies' Home Journal, May, 1972.
  STRAWBERRY POT HOLDER
  This book, Chapter VII, Plate 40.
  STRAWBERRY PINCUSHION
  This book, Chapter I, Plate 2. Directions, Chapter VII.

COUNTRY FESTIVAL (for Christmas in the Country; Old-Fashioned Christmas)

STUFFED ANIMALS

"Grandma's Barnyard," kit of four large stuffed animals to make, fabric included, $6, plus tax; "The Cleverest Things" 114 West Twenty-seventh Street, New York, New York, 10001. Also 64-page *Grandma's Barnyard Coloring Book* for resale and to sell with toys, $1 each, postpaid.

STUFFED PONY

Christmas Crafts magazine, January, 1973, page 40; $1; Countrywide Publications, 222 Park Avenue South, New York, New York 10003.

VEGETABLES AS POT HOLDERS

This book, Chapter VII, Plate 40.

VEGETABLES ON BEANBAGS AND POT HOLDERS

Seventeen Magazine's Make-It, Fall/Winter 1972, p. 79, $1; Triangle Communications, 320 Park Avenue, New York, New York 10022. Additional patterns: Lee Ward Catalog, kits of four, two kits at $1.29; item number HE 14 45634. Elgin, Illinois 60120.

VEGETABLE PILLOWS TO MAKE

"Down on the Farm," (eggplant, peapod, carrot, squash, etc.) *McCall's Needlework*, $1.25; McCall's Pattern Company, 230 Park Avenue, New York, New York 10017.

VEGETABLE CHRISTMAS ORNAMENTS

"An Embroiderer's Garden of Stitches" *McCall's* magazine, October, 1971. 230 Park Avenue, New York, New York 10017.

GINGHAM GEEGAWS (CHRISTMAS ORNAMENTS)

Woman's Day, page 67, December, 1972. Fawcett Publications, Greenwich, Connecticut 06830.

DOLLS, BAZAAR

"A Dozen Dolls from One Easy Pattern" *Woman's Day*, also Twinkie Doll and Annie Doll; also Amy Doll and her wardrobe; Woman's Day, P.O. Box 1000, Greenwich, Connecticut 06930. Also have "Mother Goose Dolls to Sew": Bo-Peep,

Boy Blue, Red Riding Hood, Square Dancers, Cowboy, Gingham Girl, etc.

DOLLS, GRANNY

To make; *Good Housekeeping Handcrafts*, Fall/Winter, 1972–73; 959 Eighth Avenue, New York, New York 10019.

DOLLS, TEEN-AGE BOLSTER

1,001 Fashion and Needlecraft Ideas, Fall/Winter, 1972; 75 cents; Conso Publishing Company, 149 Fifth Avenue, New York, New York 10010.

ROOSTER

"Cock-a-Doodle Dandy," *Woman's Day*, April, 1972. Fawcett Publications, Greenwich, Connecticut 06830.

"Rooster Felt Pillow," page 42, *Better Homes and Gardens Crafts and Sewing, 1972*, Meredith Corporation, 1716 Locust Street, Des Moines, Iowa 50336.

HEN (STRING HOLDER)

This book, Chapter II, Plate 13. Pattern from "Floribunda Fowls" project, *Golden Hands* magazine, Part 24, page 480. 6 Commercial Street, Hicksville, New York 11801.

COW (REFRIGERATOR DECORATION)

This book, Chapter VIII.

BROOMS (FIRESIDE, DECORATED)

This book, Chapter VII, Plate 51; brooms from dime store, or Strand Variety Store, Beekman Avenue, North Tarrytown, New York 10591.

PUPPETS

See Simplicity Pattern Number 9739; 85 cents.

GINGERBREAD (STUFFED DOLL FAMILY OF THREE)

Materials furnished, item number F803, The Stitchery, 204 Worcester Turnpike, Wellesley Hills, Massachusetts 02181.

GINGERBREAD MAN (STUFFED DOLL)

1,001 Fashion and Needlecraft Ideas, Fall/Winter, 1972; 75 cents; Conso Publications, 149 Fifth Avenue, New York, New York 10010.

GINGERBREAD BOY ORNAMENT

This book, Chapter IV, Plate 20.

GINGERBREAD BOY ORNAMENT

To make of needlepoint; $1.95; Victoria Gifts, 12H Water Street, Bryn Mawr, Pennsylvania 19010.

GINGERBREAD POT HOLDERS

McCall's Christmas Make-It Ideas, Volume 15, 1972. 230 Park Avenue, New York, New York 10017.

GINGERBREAD HOUSE

To make; *Woman's Day*, December, 1972, cover and page 174, Fawcett Publications, Greenwich, Connecticut 06830.

GINGERBREAD HOUSE (GRANNY'S)

Write American Molasses Company, Division of SuCrest Corporation, 120 Wall Street, New York, New York 10005. 15 cents.

RAGGEDY ANN AND ANDY

COOKIES

Good Housekeeping, December, 1971; Meredith Corporation, 1716 Locust Street, Des Moines, Iowa 50336.

DISHES FOR RESALE

$3.50 set; General Mills, Box 158, Minneapolis, Minnesota 55460.

ORNAMENTS TO MAKE

Mr. and Mrs. Ragdoll (part of a kit of six). Item number NE 14 38506, $3.79; Lee Ward Catalog, Elgin, Illinois 60120.

NEEDLEPOINT ORNAMENT TO MAKE

3½ by 5 inches; $1.95, plus 50 cents postage; Victoria Gifts, 12 H Water Street, Bryn Mawr, Pennsylvania 19010.

PATCHWORK

CHRISTMAS STOCKING

Popular Crafts, December, 1972, $1; Challenge Publications, 7950 Deering Avenue, Canoga Park, California 91304.

HOBO STICK SACHETS

Woman's Day, November, 1972, page 140; Fawcett Publications, Greenwich, Connecticut 06830.

"HOUSE-SHAPED" PILLOW

Seventeen's Make-It, Fall/Winter 1972, page 76; Triangle

Communications, 320 Park Avenue, New York, New York 10022.

STUFFED WORM TOY

Better Homes and Gardens Crafts and Sewing, 1972; $1.35; Meredith Corporation, 1716 Locust Street, Des Moines, Iowa 50336.

AIRPLANE, STUFFED TOY

Family Circle, November, 1971; 488 Madison Avenue, New York, New York 10022.

STEAMBOAT, STUFFED TOY

Family Circle, November, 1971; 488 Madison Avenue, New York, New York 10022.

DOOR WREATH

Family Circle, November, 1971; 488 Madison Avenue, New York, New York 10022.

WESTERN BOOTS CHRISTMAS STOCKINGS

Quilted patchwork "his" and "hers" stockings for Christmas; Showers Unlimited, Box 2491 North Hollywood, California 91602; $6.50 pair, plus 50 cents handling. Or make your own patterns, *Family Circle*, November, 1971.

CALICO

CHRISTMAS ORNAMENTS

This book, Chapter VII, Plate 38. Patterns (house, heart, star, fish, butterfly, etc.) also from Simplicity Number 9485.

TREE, ANGEL AND STOCKING; WREATH

Calico or patchwork, pages 38 and 39, *House and Garden*, December, 1972. 420 Lexington Avenue, New York, New York 10017.

MOUSE

This book, Chapter VI, Plate 30.

DOG AND CAT

See "Cat/Canine Bazaar" below, this chapter.

STOCKING STUFFERS

This book, Chapter VII.

WORRISOME WORM EDUCATIONAL STUFFED TOY

This book, Chapter VII, Plate 37.

DRAGON

"Creatures Who Missed the Ark," *Family Circle Holiday Helps Book, Christmas,* 1971, 99 cents. 488 Madison Avenue, New York, New York 10022.

SEASHORE PRODUCTS

ALLIGATOR

Bean bag or stuffed toy; *Woman's Day,* April, 1969. See Chapter I, also Plates 3, 3A and 3B.

CRAB

Plate 3B, this book. Pattern, page 136, *McCall's Needlework and Crafts,* Spring/Summer 1967. McCall's, 230 Park Avenue, New York, New York 10017.

FISH

Bookmark, this book, Chapter VII, see Plate 54A. *Apron with fishes, McCall's Needlework,* 1971 Springtime Issue, 230 Park Avenue, New York, New York 10017. *Goldfish,* pattern, page 79, *1,001 Fashion and Needlecraft Ideas,* Fall/Winter, 1972, Conso Publications, 149 Fifth Avenue, New York, New York 10010.

FROG

See Simplicity Pattern Number 9740. *Beanbag, Woman's Day,* April, 1969, Fawcett Publications, Greenwich, Connecticut 06830. *Chenille ball frog,* page 37, *1,001 Fashion and Needlecraft Ideas,* Spring/Summer, 1972, Conso Publications, 149 Fifth Avenue, New York, New York 10010.

LOCH NESS MONSTER

See "Dragon" under "Calico Products" above.

MERMAID

"Creatures That Missed The Ark," *Family Circle Holiday Helps,* 1971, 99 cents; (Plate 3A , this book); 488 Madison Avenue, New York, New York 10022.

OCTOPUS

Stocking stuffer, this book, Chapter VII, *Yarn, Handicraft Fun,* 69 cents, dime stores, Book Number 1639, Whitman Publishing Company, Racine, Wisconsin. *Beach bag or pattern for stuffed toy,* page 56, *1,001 Fashion and Needlecraft Ideas,* Spring/Summer, 1972; Conso Publications, 149 Fifth

Avenue, New York, New York 10010. Also, *Better Homes and Gardens*, September, 1971; Meredith Corporation, 1716 Locust Street, Des Moines, Iowa 50336.

SEA HORSE

Bookmark, this book, Chapter VII, Plate 54A.

SEAL

Beanbag, this book, Chapter VII.

Stuffed animal of terry cloth, page 136, *McCall's Needlework and Crafts*, Spring/Summer 1967. McCall's, 230 Park Avenue, New York, New York 10017.

SHELL

"Angel in Flight" *ornament*, this book, Plate 5. Directions, Chapter VII.

SNAIL

Stocking stuffer, this book, Chapter VII.

SNAKE

Chapter VI this book, Plate 27. Snake is filled with birdseed.

TURTLE

Beanbag, *Woman's Day*, April, 1969. Fawcett Publications, Greenwich, Connecticut 06830. *Stuffed toy or pillow*, Simplicity Pattern Number 9740, 75 cents.

PINE PRODUCTS

PINE-CONE MAIDENS

This book, Plate 4, directions, Chapter VII.

CYPRESS PINE-CONE TREE AND/OR MUSIC BOX

This book, Chapter VII, Plate 53.

PINE-CONE CREATIONS (IN BRANDY SNIFTER)

Page 55, *Popular Crafts*, Volume I, Number 2, December, 1972; $1. Challenge Publications, 7950 Deering Avenue, Canoga Park, California 91304.

BALSAM INCENSE

For resale; item 1100, Clymer's of Bucks County, Chestnut Street, Nashua, New Hampshire 03060. See catalog.

BALSAM PILLOWS

To make yourself, or order for resale, $1.75 for 3- × 7-inch pillow, item number 258-B, Clymer's of Buck's County, Chestnut Street, Nashua, New Hampshire 03060.

HANDCRAFTER'S TAIL-GATE BAZAAR
All handmade products listed in this book would be applicable.

ORCHARDIST'S BAZAAR
See *Strawberry and Fruit Apron*, under "Strawberry Festival"
Apron

Candied *fruit decorations* for baked goods, 75 to one box for
$1.40, item number 23876, Maid of Scandinavia Catalog,
3245 Raleigh Avenue, Minneapolis, Minnesota 55416.

Panoramic Fruits (Apple, pear, etc.), this book, Plates 57
and 58. Also see *The Trees of Christmas* by Edna Metcalfe,
Abingdon Press, Nashville, Tennessee 37219.

YOU CAN GO HOME AGAIN BAZAAR
Fruit Memo Holders, page 196, Maid of Scandinavia Catalog
to sell at profit. All calico, old-fashioned, and Down-on-the-
Farm products and books.

CAT/CANINE BAZAAR
Cat and dog, best-seller *stuffed toys*; Simplicity Pattern Number 9740.

Autograph Hound stuffed dog, The Sewing Basket, September,
1972; Volume 3, Number 14, Cherlton Publications, Division
Street, Derby, Connecticut 06418.

The 3 Cat and Kittens, stuffed toys, November, 1972, *Woman's
Day*, Greenwich, Connecticut 06830.

Cat-in-the-Garden, pages 83 and 153, *Good Housekeeping
Needlecraft*, 1971, 959 Eighth Avenue, New York, New York
10019.

Hound dog toy to knit, page 15, *Christmas Crafts* magazine,
January, 1973, $1. Countrywide Publications, 222 Park
Avenue South, New York, New York 10003.

Wide-eyed puppy with rope legs, Good Housekeeping Booklet
Number 801, 75 cents, Good Housekeeping Bulletin Services,
959 Eighth Avenue, New York, New York 10019.

Dog and cat cookie cutters, see Maid of Scandinavia and
Wilton catalogs.

STARS AND STRIPES BAZAAR

See *"Treetop Star"* of milkweed pods, this book, Plate 4, Chapter I.

See *Calico Ornament Star*, Plate 39, this book.

Star cookie cutters, Maid of Scandinavia Catalog. See catalogs.

Star of gift-wrap cord. Page 67, *Woman's Day*, December, 1972. Fawcett Publications, Greenwich, Connecticut 06830.

Star cakepan, Texas cookie cutter, United States map cake or pie pan, Maid of Scandinavia Catalog. See catalogs.

Baking decorations of flags, package of 8 at 35 cents, Maid of Scandinavia Catalog. See Catalogs.

Betsy Ross music box to sell at profit, or make your own (plays "God Bless America") from Maid of Scandinavia Catalog. See Catalogs.

MOM AND APPLE PIE BAZAAR

See most of above ideas under "Stars and Strips Bazaar," including all gift products for a woman; sachets, cookie cutters, pot holders, night-light lady, etc. Also, apple pie, taffy apples, etc.

Products Suitable for Use in Bazaars Described in Chapter II

EASTER BAZAAR

EASTER TREES TO SELL

Chapter II, this book, Plates 8 and 9. How to make tree pots, Chapter IX.

PANORAMIC EGGS

Chapter VIII, this book, Plates 56–58.

EASTER MUSIC BOXES

Chapter IV, this book, Plates 42–43.

EGG COZY

Back cover, *Golden Hands* magazine, Volume 2, Part 17, 95 cents. 6 Commercial Street, Hicksville, New York 11801.

EASTER BASKET EARRINGS

Chapter VII, this book, Plate 59. Baskets from Children's Department, The Village Gallery, 1 Croton Point Avenue, Croton-on-Hudson, New York 10520. Also used to hold bouquet of flowers on Easter egg trees.

KNITTED EASTER BASKET

This book, Chapter VII, Plate 54.

EASTER PURSE

This book, Chapter VII, Plate 53A.

DUCK PENCIL CASE

This book, Chapter VII, Plate 53A.

NIGHT-LIGHT LADY

This book, Chapter VII, Plate 41.

BUTTERFLY LIGHT-SWITCH COVER

This book, Chapter VII. Also patterns for tulip and mushroom, page 58, *Better Homes and Gardens Crafts and Sewing*, 1972, $1.35; Meredith Corporation, 1716 Locust Street, Des Moines, Iowa 50336.

BUTTERFLY POT HOLDER

Page 47, *Better Homes and Gardens Crafts and Sewing*, 1972, $1.35; Meredith Corporation, 1716 Locust, Des Moines, Iowa 50336.

BUTTERFLY FLYSWATTER

This book, Chapter VIII.

BIRD AND NEST

Of chenille balls; pages 59, 94, and 95, *1,001 Fashion and Needlework Ideas*, Spring/Summer 1972. Conso Publishing Corporation, 149 Fifth Avenue, New York, New York 10010.

LADYBUG

This book, Chapter VI, Plate 26.

CENTIPEDES

This book, Chapter VI, Plate 25.

CATERPILLAR

Or "Draft-Dodger." See Plate 36. Pattern from *Family Circle Special Christmas Projects*, 1970. 488 Madison Avenue, New York, New York 10022.

PETER RABBIT DISHES

For resale. Melamineware (plate fruit bowl, cup, and cereal bowl); $3.50 set; General Mills, Box 158, Minneapolis, Minnesota 55460.

246

WOODLAND BUNNY SCENE IN LARGE EGG
Item K13E, $7.52; show-stopping bazaar item, see Plate 12, this book. The Pink Sleigh, Oldwick, New Jersey 08858.

PANORAMIC EGG WITH STANDS
Holiday Handicrafts, Winsted, Connecticut 06098. Blue, pink, yellow, 39 cents set. Item number A151. Excellent bazaar seller.

BOUTIQUE EGGS TO MAKE
Kits with instructions. J. Tickey, 5532 North Persimmon Avenue, Temple City, California 91780.

SMALL AND LARGE EGGS FOR EASTER TREES
See Plates 8 and 9, this book. Supplies from the Pink Sleigh, Oldwick, New Jersey 08858. Also sells tree branches and tree trunks. See Pink Sleigh catalog.

TULIP-TIME STRUNG PARTY LIGHTS (DECORATION)
By Patio Products, $7.99. Helen Gallagher Foster Catalog, North Galena Road, Peoria, Illinois 61614. Also, Macy's, Herald Square, New York, New York.

BUNNY
Beanbag. Woman's Day, April, 1969, Fawcett Publications, Greenwich, Connecticut 06830.

BUNNY
Stuffed toy, "This Bunny's a Honey," *Golden Hands* magazine, 95 cents, page 74, Part 4, 6 Commercial Street, Hicksville, New York, 11801.

BUNNY AND ELEPHANT COOKIES
This book, Chapter IV.

RABBITS AND ORANGE-JUICE CAN
This book, Plates 20 and 21, Chapter IV.

JET-DRY BASKET PRODUCTS
This book, Plate 28, Chapter VI.

SKUNK WITH PERFUME
This book, Chapter VIII, Plate 65.

MA AND PA HIPPO
See Plate 11, this book. Pattern from Simplicity Pattern Number 8951.

See Plate 40, this book. Patterns, Chapter VII.

Strawberry, vegetable, in-the-country products, as well as many seashore products, also applicable to Easter/spring bazaar.

Books and Sources for Egg Decoration for Boutiques and Bazaars

GETTING STARTED IN EGG DECORATION
By Nancy Lang, $2.95; Bruce Publishing Company, 866 Third Avenue, New York, New York 10022.

THE SPLENDID ART OF DECORATING EGGS
By Rosemary Dinney, $10; Hearthside Press, 445 Northern Boulevard, Great Neck, New York 11021.

EGGER'S GAZETTE
Published free several times a year by Taylor House, Bench and Perry Streets, Galena, Illinois 61036.

"MONEY GROWS ON HER EASTER EGG TREES"
Family Circle Book of Careers at Home by Mary Bass Gibson, $5.95; Family Circle Books, Department 434, P.O. Box 450, Teaneck, New Jersey 07666.
Creative Crafts magazine April, 1971; 50 cents plus postage. 31 Arch Street, Ramsay, New Jersey 07446.
Hollow eggs of white plastic for bazaar decoration or découpage. Lee Ward Catalog, Elgin, Illinois 60120.

CHRISTMAS AROUND THE WORLD BAZAAR
  IDEAS FOR INTERNATIONAL PRODUCTS
See "Make It a Merry Christmas," pages 8, 9, 10, *Popular Crafts* magazine, December, 1972, $1; Challenge Publications, 7950 Deering Avenue, Canoga Park, California 91304.
See *Christmas Around the World*, $1.75; Ideals Publication, 11315 Watertown Plank Road, Milwaukee, Wisconsin 53226.
See *Christmas the World Over* by Daniel J. Foley, $5.95; Chilton Book Company, New York, New York.

See Brochure from "1225" Shop, 745 Alexander Road, Princeton, New Jersey 07009.

CHRISTMAS-IN-THE-COUNTRY BAZAAR
Read *An Old Fashioned Christmas by Paul Engle*, $3.95; The Dial Press, 730 Third Avenue, New York, New York 10017. See brochure from Homespun Products, Route 1, Gastonia, North Carolina 28052.
See "Herbs and Herb Products" under "Catalogs," above.
See Blue Ridge Hearthside Crafts Catalog.

MINI-BAZAAR
See "Christmas Around the World Bazaar" above.
See Program Ideas—"A Church Herald Meeting Plan" and Kit, available from The Church Herald, 630 Myrtle Street, Grand Rapids, Michigan 49504.

GARAGE SALE
If baked goods are added to the sale, consider the decorations, gay but all-purpose, such as "smiley faces" picks, 12 to a set, at 55 cents, item number 91847, Maid of Scandinavia Catalog. Or miniature balloons in a bunch, 6 bunches at 65 cents, item number 95230, Maid of Scandinavia Catalog, 3245 Raleigh Avenue, Minneapolis, Minnesota 55416.

Additional Information Pertinent to Topics Discussed in Chapter IV

I LIKE CHRISTMAS BOOK
35 cents, The Abbey Press, St. Meinrad, Indiana 47577. Excellent to sell with other products such as stuffed toys.

MORE UNUSUAL RECIPES
Mountaineer and hill country recipes: Homespun Products Catalog, Route 1, Gastonia, North Carolina 28052.

ADDITIONAL STAINED GLASS RECIPE
Stained Glass Fruitcake: 25 cents, Mrs. Arlene Born, Rte. 1, Adell, Wisconsin 53001.

NEW BAZAAR THEME
Recipes for 200-year United States commemorative celebration—

many of these recipes served when the United States became a nation, $4.95, plus 50 cents postage; U.S. Commemorative Cook Book, P.O. Box 9057, Kansas City, Missouri 64168. Also excellent theme for a bazaar.

Additional Information Pertinent to Topics Discussed in Chapter VIII

RECYCLED OR ECOLOGICAL PRODUCTS TO MAKE
See Christ Child in the walnut shell ornament, Christmas choir of acorns, products of riverbed stones (Pebble People), hair-conditioner bottle ornaments (Fermadyl: Fermadyl Labs, Los Angeles, California; products used in Saks department store and other beauty shops), recycled computer tape ring ornaments, recycled Jet-Dry basket products, paper tube Christmas tree decoration. Also milkweed pod, sweet-gum and pine-cone products listed herein.

Additional Information Pertinent to Topics Discussed in Chapter IX

SANTA PRODUCTS
Santa dolls, see Plate 47, this book. "Heigh-Ho Santas; 3 patterns to make; *Woman's Day*, December, 1970; Fawcett Publications, Greenwich, Connecticut 06830.
Ornaments to make: "Little Faces of Wooden Spoons", page 66, *Woman's Day*, December, 1972, Fawcett Publications, Greenwich, Connecticut 06830. Also page 175, December, 1972, *Woman's Day*, as above.
Santa boot, see Plate 66, this book.
Pattern, $1, Leland of Reseda, Reseda, California 91335, includes three variations.

* See Chapter X, Maid of Scandinavia Catalog.

INDEX

251